MAMA SAID, THIS BOY IS GONNA BE SOMEBODY!

The Untold Story
of
Oklahoma Blues Legend D.C. Minner

MONGREL EMPIRE PRESS
NORMAN, OKLAHOMA, UNITED STATES OF AMERICA

2018

FIRST EDITION, 2018

Mama Said, 'This Boy's Gonna Be Somebody!'
The Untold Story of Oklahoma Blues Legend D.C. Minner
© 2018 by La Nelda Hughes and Selby Minner

ISBN 978-1-7323935-1-6

Cover Art & Design
© 2018 by Selby Minner

MONGREL EMPIRE PRESS
NORMAN, OK

ONLINE CATALOGUE: WWW.MONGRELEMPIRE.ORG

This publisher is a proud member of

COUNCIL OF LITERARY MAGAZINES & PRESSES
W W W . C L M P . O R G

MAMA SAID, THIS BOY IS GONNA BE SOMEBODY!

The Untold Story
of
Oklahoma Blues Legend D.C. Minner

by La Nelda Hughes
with D.C. Minner and Selby Minner

and notes from Dr. Harold Aldridge and many more

CONTENTS

Foreword

WHY SHOULD WE CARE ABOUT D.C.'S STORY?

John Bailey of Norman, Oklahoma, a mechanic, worked on Selby's van several times while D.C. was hospitalized during his final illness. Bailey told Selby, "We haven't known D.C. long," he said, "but he's had a big impact on our lives. I feel like he's a very bright light, like a comet going by, and everyone he's touched will have a brighter life."

The story of D.C. Minner is like a self-help book; most of this book is in D.C.'s words. Among D.C.'s most endearing characteristics was his determination to use the lessons learned from his own experiences and his music to help kids stay out of trouble and make the best lives possible for themselves. He would say, "The music will lead you to drugs and drinking so you have to hold tight to the music and it will also pull out of those situations... you don't want to get off the train in the middle of the tunnel." He not only knew how to reach the young; he was also eager to share that knowledge.

"We don't expect them to become great musicians, we teach them courage. We specialize in teaching the kids others have thrown away," D.C. said. "We work with the troublemakers. We go into schools where some people are scared of the kids. I get their teachers out of the room so that I can pull the kids out of their usual behaviors and can teach them something. Music is a hook to get their attention. What we leave them with is courage. When we leave, they're different kids. They have more self-esteem," he said. "We give them the courage to try, to sing in front of their peers—not easy, and we include them in the band with us. Then we teach them they can spend that courage on other things, as well as on music."

D.C. knew to be specific and to give his listeners or readers something they could use. He taught people how to take control of their lives by weaving his advice into absorbing stories.

But D.C.'s wisdom has value that goes far beyond his work with children. He was a successful and respected black man from the South in a good (and long) marriage with a liberated white woman from the North. In his words, he has grandchildren "in all hues." The knowledge he gained from this can help to smooth relationships between races and to aid people who deal with diverse groups. What he learned from his own grandmother and what he learned himself with his own grandchildren can inspire grandparents who want to make a difference in children's lives. His wisdom from living a long life and meeting the challenges of it head-on can prepare people to accept old age. What he learned from the music industry can tutor people who want to succeed in the world of entertainment or in other fields.

"When D.C. talks you have to listen—not just because he speaks so quietly, but because it seems like something you'll want to remember," said Jack Fowler, a fellow musician who was the editor of Checotah's *McIntosh County Democrat*. "What he says is something you will want to keep with you."

"These are wonderful teachings to give to the world," said Julie Moss, a family friend from Tahlequah. As Blues Hall of Fame board member, part time back up vocalist in the Minner band and the wife of a blues musician, Moss had many chances to see D.C. at work. "There was great depth and substance to the bluesman we all know and love, more to him than met the eye. He was like a fascinating story book. He had the calm in the face of the storms of life to see beyond them with a special vision, dignity, and clarity of purpose."

"Most people seem to be walking around in a dream state," D.C. said. "Actually a dream is a wonderful thing. Everything starts with a dream. But a dream by itself is like a jellyfish. It has no structure. It's hard to maintain any shape to it. But when you add a plan to a dream, you have structure for your dream. That plan will tell you how to get from point A to point B to point C.

I tell kids, when you put a plan and a dream together, you come up with something called a scheme. A scheme is part dream, but it also has a practical way to get to it; one foot in the clouds and one foot firmly planted on the ground. I tell them, "You can hang out and go where the winds take you, but you won't like the result."

D.C. was fond of telling listeners that he made it from a "house of shame," the corner bar where he was reared in a religious town, to four Halls of Fame (the Oklahoma Jazz Hall of Fame, the Oklahoma Blues Hall of Fame, the Oklahoma Music Hall of Fame, the Payne County Line Hall of Fame). He pointed out that he was from a town with a population of less than a hundred people. "If I can do it, they can do it," he said.

When D.C. talked, as a friend, mentor or philosopher, people generally listened. His dignity, his self-confidence, the melodious voice he used with great skill, his storytelling knowhow, his humor, his poise and comfort before an audience, his genuine warmth, his erect bearing, and a handsome face refined by adversity: all were parts of a personality that pulled people to him. Some call that charisma. Added to that, people responded to D.C. because they felt their importance to him. He let them know that. "The love he gave was really extraordinary," Selby said. "It was very powerful. He remembered them all by name."

"My job in life is to run in front and kick the rocks out of the road, the ones that I know about that some others might not can (sic) see," D.C. said about his work. He had ample reason to know about the value of planning one's life, and those lessons did not come to him easily, as his story has revealed. But, if the recognition and awards that came his way are any indication, he got it right.

A Self-Made Man

LaNelda Hughes, author of this book, came to Rentiesville because her husband Don wanted to learn bass. The night the book starts, D.C. was being inducted to the Oklahoma Music Hall of Fame. Brooks and Dunn were on the show as well because Ronnie Brooks was also inducted. They had ten years of number-one hits on the Western Music charts. Their production required two semis and two huge highway buses and a truck with an immense generator. The setup included 14 guitars on the stage before the band came on, each with remotes. Four marines in dress whites stood at attention during their patriotic number and confetti cannons filled the civic center with foot long red white and blue streamers as the show came to a close. They played for an hour. Four-thousand people came to the OMHOF inductions–by far the largest crowd they had ever drawn for this event. D.C.'s show was 15 minutes as was that of Flash Terry and the rest of the inductees. D.C. hit the stage ready. LaNelda's husband sat in on one song on bass and Selby played that one on guitar. The crowd rose to their feet 4 times during that 15 minute set. The audience was proud of this local man of color. His work in the community touched their hearts and they wanted him to know. They wanted the Hall of Fame to know. They were not all his fans—most came for Brooks and Dunn—but they knew him and gave him their best. Selby said "Four standing ovations from four-thousand people in fifteen minutes. I will never forget it as long as I live."

Not long after the induction ceremony, D.C. and Selby started the Oklahoma Blues Hall of Fame in Rentiesville. D.C. said "They are going to miss some of these blues people. They have their hands full, both the Oklahoma Jazz Hall of Fame and the Oklahoma Music Hall of fame. We know them (the blues musicians) all and we have a place. We need to do something for them while they are alive. You know, you wake up one morning and you have gotten old and you have no health care maybe, and no retirement, and you say to yourself 'what did I do?' Having these trophies and knowing that in a hundred years my grandchildren can go and see my photo on the wall or that some little black kid from a small town can say ' if he came from a town of 99 people and made it to the hall of fame, than I know I can DO something too!'"

D.C. actually morphed the "house of shame" into a Hall of Fame!

This book would not be possible without countless recordings from which many quotes and stories were transcribed. The largest collection of these were recorded by Harold Aldridge, blues singer, guitarist and retired psychology professor from Northeastern State University in Tahlequah. Many thanks to Sareca Wilson at Oklahoma State University in Okmulgee and Dr. Jennifer Kidney at the University of Oklahoma for tireless work editing. Also, thanks to Selby Minner for providing resource material from the OBHOF archive and for editing. And most importantly, thanks to LaNelda Hughes for spending seven years writing this book and also to her husband, Don Hughes (pictured below).

CHAPTER 1: FAMILY & RENTIESVILLE

What's He Gonna Be, Lura?

On November 20, 2003, friends, family, and fans gathered at the Down Home Blues Club in Rentiesville to honor bluesman D.C. Minner, who was being inducted into the Oklahoma Music Hall of Fame. The club, formerly known as the Cozy Corner, an illegal corn whiskey house of the thirties, was also the home of D.C. and his wife Selby. On this evening it was filled with guests in tuxedos and glittering gowns who were seated in folding chairs or in Naugahyde-sofa booths facing the stage where the presentation was taking place. Lining the walls around the room were smoky posters and autographed photos of blues musicians from around the world who seemed to be smiling their pleasure of D.C.'s mark on the world of blues music.

A petite, glamorously-dressed woman got the attention of the crowd and then turned to the man at the center of the celebration. "D.C.," his mother-in-law Dortha Guenther said firmly, looking up into his eyes, "you know you were not my first choice as a husband for my daughter." The low chatter in the room died down as D.C.'s family members and closest friends listened closer.

"Yes ma'am, I know that," he replied gently. The long earring in his left ear and ringed right hand reflecting the stage lights were no match to the brilliance of D.C's smile. His blue hat, the blue of his shirt, the trim on his tux, the gleam of the pure white goatee on his black face, his bejeweled cummerbund—D.C

1

shined, just as he did every time he went on stage. Dortha Selby Guenther Mershon smiling with genuine affection said with the accent and assurance of a transplanted New Englander, "But I've come to love you, and I'm so happy to see you receiving this honor."

Ironically, the words spoken by Selby's mother rang true in so many ways. These words could have been speaking for the people of D.C.'s hometown. These words could have been speaking for his home state. These words could have been speaking for the blues music industry. He might not have been the first choice, but if his influences could be measured, they would show the heights he achieved in music, in education, and in winning the love of thousands of admirers.

Yet D.C. was the first choice for the most influential person in D.C.'s life. His grandmother Lura (pronounced by the family, *Lur'ee*) Martin Pearson Drennan, always insisted, to everybody who would listen, that the fat dark-skinned child who lived with her at the Cozy Corner was something special.

"That boy's gonna be somebody!" she said over and over.

"What's he gonna be, Lura?" many people asked the barkeeper.

"I don't know, but I know he's gonna be somebody."

Moving the Gene Pool to the Promised Land

The story D.C. knew about his family's origins began early in the twentieth century when his ancestors decided, as he put it, to get their gene pool out of the Old South to a place where they could reasonably expect to have a better life than the one they had lived in Alabama after the Civil War. Indian Territory, where no "Jim Crow" laws were on the books to keep blacks from voting, where blacks were treated as equals, was the place most had heard about. Between 1890 and 1910, the black population in the Territory increased as much as 600 percent; more than fifty all-black towns were established there, and blacks could vote in Indian Territory. Recruiters suggested a new state,

2

controlled by blacks, might be formed. Meanwhile, Native Americans wanted Indian Territory to come into the U.S. as an Indian state. Both groups sent delegations to Washington.

In 1900, D.C.'s great-great-grandmother, Ann Martin, was one of four Cherokee Indian sisters who were married to black men living in Chocalaca, near Lake Eufaula (Alabama) and the border with southern Georgia. When Ann Martin's first grandchild, Lura Eufaula, was born to Ann's daughter Minnie Martin Gaye in 1900, the time seemed right for the family to make a move. "They wanted to take that baby out of the South and to a new Promised Land," D.C. was told. Ann and her husband, Clark Martin, a pharmacist and businessman, were influenced by recruiters who were looking for qualified blacks to help settle planned black townships in Indian Territory.

Another factor in Ann's willingness to uproot her family and move to Indian Territory was that she had family members in the area. Some of her Cherokee ancestors had been forced there some 50 years earlier on the Trail of Tears. In addition, she knew about a third of the people who came on the Trail of Tears were black, making Indian Territory a place where mixed-race families might be accepted.

Clark Martin loaded his family, including his grandchild Lura, and possessions in covered wagons and headed west. Ann Martin's three sisters, their husbands and families, and several other families from eastern Alabama moved to Oklahoma Territory in 1901. Lura's parents, however, stayed behind.

The family found the friendlier culture they were looking for in the Creek Nation, at the location that is now the black township of Rentiesville. They were not allowed to live with Ann's relatives in the Cherokee Nation, whose capitol is Tahlequah, because the Cherokees refused to accept mixed marriages. The Seminoles and the Creeks did, however, so the Martins and their relatives settled on the edge of Creek Nation, which was as close to the Cherokees as they could get. Every chance she had, Ann Martin would ride horseback to see her family in the Cherokee Nation.

Clark Martin soon had drugstores in Rentiesville and in Eufaula, and the family prospered. Martin's customers took to calling him Doctor Clark and relied heavily on his medical advice. Martin rode a train on the Katy Railroad every day to Eufaula to oversee that store, leaving Ann and granddaughter Lura to handle the one in Rentiesville. Lura's earliest memories were of being in the store, which contributed to her lifelong entrepreneurial attributes.

Since 1911, D.C.'s family has had businesses of various kinds in Rentiesville. D.C.'s cousin Ruby Perkins, who was about twenty years older than D.C. had many memories of a once-thriving community. The town was built around a square, with sidewalks made of wooden planks. Rentiesville had a train station, with trains stopping there morning and evening. The town also had a three-story school building with about 200 students, two drug stores (one owned by D.C.'s great-great-grandfather), a shoe store, a restaurant and rooming house, a pool hall, four churches, a cotton gin, a grist mill, a post office, a town well, a jail, a town marshal, an undertaker with a coffin factory, and a grocery store. The Rentiesville Fair was a three-day event with food, livestock judging, and horse races.

In 1907, Oklahoma became a state and Rentiesville became a chartered town. When D. C. Minner tore down the homestead on his property in the 1980s, he found a cornerstone that listed the founders of Rentiesville as Bill Rentie, D. C. Martin, Julius Morris and Rev. N. A. Robinson.

In 1915 Lura Martin married Tom Pearson with whom she had three daughters: Ethel, Helen (D.C's mother), and Elsie. Lura continued helping her grandfather in his businesses after she married and had children. About all D.C. remembered knowing about Pearson was that he was from Louisiana and that he taught Lura to make milk pie by rolling out a crust, cutting up pieces of butter over it, then pouring milk and sugar over it and baking it. D.C. was very surprised, many years later when he was in France, to find milk pie there, exactly as he remembered it from Lura's kitchen in Oklahoma.

4

In the 1920s, even though Tulsa's so-called race riot in its all-black community resulted in at least 3,000 blacks killed, about 1,500 homes burned, and every business destroyed, in Rentiesville, life was good and otherwise uneventful for the Martins' extended family. Then, Doctor Clark, the principal breadwinner, died in 1927. Shortly afterward, the Great Depression brought hardships for almost everyone, and especially for the mixed Cherokee/black Martin family whose strongest member was gone. The family lost everything. Then, Lura's husband, Tom, left the family during the same period.

"My grandmother Lura found herself down here with three daughters and no income," D. C. said. "Her pillar of support, Clark Martin, was dead. The family's nest egg was gone. There were a lot of cousins with her also. Hard times had hit all of them, so they all had got used to coming to my great-grandma's house to get stuff." D.C.'s grandmother Lura worked, chopping cotton, for thirty-five cents per day to try to keep her family together. "But they were starving to death down here on this corner," D.C. said. "The kids were scraping their plates trying to get enough food. There was no place to turn for help."

Lura and her three daughters formed a little singing group and performed in the First Baptist Church in Rentiesville. Lura and all three daughters sang; Elsie played piano, and Lura played accordion, although she didn't use it in the church. They were in the church every time the doors were open. But, with everybody in the area also suffering economic hard times, their situation was desperate.

"There were holes in their house where people driving by could look in and see them eating dinner," D. C. said. "The family could see the sky through holes in the roof. When storms came through, they would push all the furniture against the door and lean on it to keep the wind from blowing the door open. But, others in town were having hard times as well. In later years, when they could joke about it, people in town would say of one of the families that their members were so hungry their mother would hang a piece of bacon rind on a string by the door. Each kid would swallow it on the way out to school every morning, then the mother would pull it back up, so that at least 'their insides were greased.'"

"And then it was that a guy by the name of Sam Durham came here to Rentiesville," D. C. recalled his grandmother saying. "He had been down to the penitentiary at one time or another. He was a gambler and a street person. He caught my grandmother's eye, and he taught her to make Choctaw beer. A little potatoes or grain, yeast and sugar, and in four or five days, you have beer."

A year or two later, Charlie Drennan became her boyfriend. He had a check from the VA because he had suffered a stroke while in the service.

Having had the entrepreneurial experience in the drugstore, my grandmother knew how to sell things. She soon figured out what the profit margin would be, she could see she could make money. My grandmother said, 'Oh, my God! I can get money to feed my kids with this recipe.' She took that check and went into business. She began selling the Choctaw (aka choc) beer, as well as locally made bootlegged corn whiskey, to get money to feed her family."

Lura made a covenant with God at the beginning. "She asked the Lord if he would help her and protect her, until she got her children (and later grandson D.C.) raised, she would quit selling the alcohol when her last child left home, only sell beer, and never do anything else illegal in her life," D. C. said. "Beginning the day I left home to join the Army, she never sold another drop. She never did another thing illegal. I don't mean the day after. I mean the very day! She said, 'A deal is a deal'. All those years that she had bootlegged, she never got busted or went to jail or nothing."

But everybody in town turned against her.

1935 D.C. Makes His Entry

D.C. Minner was born January 28, 1935, to Helen Pearson Minner and Clarence Minner when Helen was seventeen on land the family had owned since 1915 in Rentiesville. Of his parents' marriage, D.C. said, "It was a shotgun marriage, and it lasted about six weeks. Their mothers were instrumental in the break up. One was Baptist and the other Holy Roller, and they didn't get along." D.C. was raised by his maternal grandmother, Lura Martin Pearson, who had been brought to up there by her grandparents, Dr. Clark and Ann Martin.

Lura, who had always wanted a son, told her young daughter, "You've already made one mistake, having this baby so young. Don't make another one—give the boy to me to raise and go start your life over. Go have some fun!" He was given the name Doctor Clark at birth, after the grandfather that Lura revered. The young boy got his name legally changed to D.C. as soon as he was old enough. "I was already black and fat," he said. "That was enough handicaps for any kid, without having to constantly explain that name."

When D.C. was a few weeks old, he became dangerously ill. Lura called the doctor, Pinkie Durham, who was also the mailman and lived down the road across from the Baptist Church. According to the family story, the doctor said, "Lura, that boy is goin' to die."

"Get out of my house!" D.C.'s grandmother demanded. "I didn't call you to tell me that. I called you to help me get him better." She then put D.C. on a pillow on her lap and began to rub quinine and hog lard on him. She continued to hold and caress him all night. When anyone tried to move him to somebody else's lap, he would start to fuss. So Lura held on to him and refused to let the baby die.

Much later in his life, after D.C. studied the ancient Indian sacred spiritual science taught by Paramahansa Yogananda, he developed a theory about how his grandmother managed to save his life when he was an infant. "Neither of my parents wanted a baby," D C. said about the incident. "Their families didn't want them to have a baby. Those kids were not settled enough to hold me there. I didn't want to be there and was ready to go. But when my grandmother showed me the love she did, she willed me to live. I felt her and decided to stay on earth. A close bond was established that night.

"I was very attached to her, not to anybody else, for a long time because "she raised me in this corn whiskey house. I was born in it. My baby auntie (Elsie, about fourteen at the time) had the responsibility of doing motherly duties like changing diapers and feeding me. My grandmother was in charge, though."

Life with Lura and the people who came in and out of that house shaped D.C. Sam Durham, the man who taught Lura to make the illegal beer that supported her family, died of lung disease while D. C. was small. But he was later told that Durham tested him when he was very young. Durham put a pair of dice and some money in front of the little boy and said, "Let's see which one he chooses."

"I was told that I went toward the money, instead of picking up the dice," D. C. said. "He said, 'Well, he won't be a gambler.'" Several of Durham's stepchildren lived with the family while D. C. was growing up. Some were musicians who had an influence on D. C.

One of those who lived with D. C.'s grandmother, Willie Durham, played guitar. When she grew up, she hopped a train with her young child out of Rentiesville to go play music for a living. D.C. ran into her years later when all of them were performing in Oklahoma City. She had married a musician and had a family band.

"Another one of them was Lucius Durham," he said. "We called him L. D. or Old Grey Eyes. He was a big boy and he could play piano." D.C. remembered sitting on L. D.'s lap at the piano, from the age of two. "He later taught me the arrangement of "Key to the Highway" that I use to this day," D.C. said in his seventies.

"I was on that piano all day long, to the point where they took the piano out of the house and set it outside. I was still on it all day long on the front porch. They literally destroyed it. They made it into a piece of furniture where you could keep cakes and pies in it. Called it a pie safe. I was not encouraged to be a musician because musicians were people of low stature. They called a guitar a 'starvation box.' My grandmother intended for me to be a doctor. But that didn't stop me," D.C. said. "Every time I ran into a piano, I'd sit down and try to play it. I guess I always wanted to play music."

When D.C. was a child, he would often sing when he was sent outside to play by himself. Sometimes he would get under the window near where his grandmother was working and sing, "I'm soo lone–some, I'm soo lonesome . . ." His grandmother would then tell him, "You better stop that! You better stay outside and make yourself a play-pretty!"

"I used to listen to a lot of radio," D.C. told interviewers George Carney and Hugh Foley for a feature story in *Living Blues* magazine. "We'd come in from the fields and the old man would listen to the news and to Bob Wills and the Texas Playboys. There was no talking while we listened because it was a dry cell battery radio, and you could only turn it on so long. Bob Wills' music was the first time I ever heard horns in a band. I thought that was the best music I ever heard. I liked all that Bob Wills music. I liked the steel guitar.

"After Sam died, my grandmother became involved with another man, Charlie Drennan. Charlie had been in World War I, and he'd been disabled while in the Navy. He had a disability check coming. He let my grandmother manage that check. That's what rescued us from dire straits, was his pension. That little steady money was all Miss Lura needed to go into business. First, she opened a dance hall with a Victrola. We got another house. She bought the whole block of land where we live now, and it was no more scraping of (the silverware against) the plates."

Later in her life, Lura could not bear the sound of a fork or spoon scraping on a dish, as it reminded her of her family's near-starvation. She would say, "Go get yourself some more food."

D.C. Learns Music Excites People

D.C. got his first exposure to live music when Elsie, who had the day-to-day job of looking after him, wanted to go to community dances held out in the fields away from town.

"'It's all right with me,' my grandmother would say, 'but you have to take him (D.C.) with you,'" D.C. remembered. "I was a little fat baby, a fat kid all my life. She would have to carry me. I couldn't walk three or four miles. So some of her young friends would take turns putting me on their shoulders and carrying me."

The revelers would go out into the countryside away from town because of the noise of the music. "People worked so hard," D. C. said. "They would bust you for disturbing the peace. The organizers would clear off a place, string some lights (lit rags stuffed in soft drink bottles full of kerosene), and get some musicians going in one area and gambling in another. You'd have a blanket spread out where four or five babies would be on it, a nursery-type situation. Just a big party out in the woods. That was my first taste of parties, I guess, and music, live music!"

After a while, his grandmother saw the value of adding live music to her business. D.C. remembered hearing guitars, fiddles, and accordions playing dance music. "Waltzes were popular as was western swing, lots of Bob Wills' songs," he said. "The faster pieces were called stomp music. Men often danced by themselves to these, sometimes called 'buck dancing.'" Popular country blues songs included "Corrine, Corrina" and "Sittin' on Top of the World."

"I saw how excited my aunties and grandmother would get when they knew the musicians were coming," D. C. said. "They'd take all the furniture out of the house. They'd scrub the floors with soapy water and brushes and bleach and lye. Then that pine floor, over a period of time, would develop a white nap when it dried. Then they would put the furniture back in, get all dressed up, and they were ready for the party.

"That excited me. I wanted to learn how to play that guitar so I could excite my grandmother and others like that," he said. "I wanted that power. I saw how much they liked that music and I wanted to be able to give that to them. I loved them so much. "Well, when the musicians got a little bit more to drink than they needed, they would lay the guitars down and kinda doze off. Then I would automatically go over, get a guitar, carry it back to my room and try to play it, but it wouldn't sound right. I was about five or six at the time.

"I was a pretty smart little boy. I knew when it didn't sound right, they would start turning things on the machines. So I thought I'd twist on the machines, too. And a string would go 'pop'! I'd say 'uh, oh.' I'd take that guitar out of there and lay it back down by the drunk. That worked a couple of times, but one day the guy woke up. He said, 'Lura, if you don't keep that little fat boy away from my guitar, we're goin' to stop comin' down here.' So that was the end of that. But I listened every time they came. They got replaced anyway in the early forties."

D.C.'s first exposure to recorded music was a Victrola. When he was about four years old, before he could read, he could pick out the records people requested by their labels, and put them on the Victrola and wind it up just right.

Then, "We got a jukebox when the power came," D.C. said. A rural cooperative brought electricity to the area during World War II. "This huge pretty box was in the corner of my house. It changed colors constantly and played amplified music. I realize now I'd never heard amplified music before. So BIG the sound was!" Customers would give him change and say, "Play me something good now!"

"I knew what number every song was," he said. "I knew all the songs by the look of the labels; I was 'picture-reading'. I've been picking songs people want to hear for a very long time. That became what I did for a living. The music played at the

11

Cozy Corner was everything from old breakdowns to Delta blues. Chuck Berry was our rock 'n roll."

"I really loved that box," D.C. said. "We called it a 'venda' (possibly because it was serviced by a vendor). I had an idea there were little people inside playing that music. That made sense to me. I told Mama Lura, 'I want to be in there,' meaning I wanted to make music," D.C. remembered. "She would say, 'Oh, no baby, you can't get in there.' I'd still think to myself, 'I'm going to get in there.' And I did."

Similarly to D.C.'s imaginative wish, Selby had an idea about how music was made. As a four year old child in Rhode Island, she got her first record player. It opened up like a little suitcase and played 45 rpm records. "It was the most fascinating toy I'd ever seen," Selby said. "I imagined little tiny people inside the bottom of the record player, all playing instruments and singing. I wanted very badly to get inside there with them, but of course I was too big. I just lay on the floor, listening and switching records, until my mother made me stop to come and eat."

Later, after Selby and D.C. had gotten together, D.C. remembered, "The first time I walked into a place where one of our records was playing on the jukebox. I turned to Selby and said, 'See, I did get into that jukebox after all!' Selby said, 'I got in there, too!' They were playing our first CD, 'Love Lost and Found.' But my grandmother didn't see it. She was dead by the time I got inside the jukebox."

"A man named Grant Smith would come from Muskogee to rob the jukebox," D.C. said. "I'd be right there watching. I always had a lot of questions for him. He'd pour that money out on our kitchen table. It would be more money than I'd ever seen anywhere else. We'd count it all up and stack it up and put it in those rolls. Then he'd give my grandmother half and he'd take half. Then we'd put new records on.

"By that time, my mother and Aunt Ethel had gone to the cities. My grandmother Lura, Aunt Elsie, and I would have to decide what new records to put on. Sometimes Grant Smith would want to take one off and we'd say, 'No! That's one of our good ones. Aw, no, you can't take THAT off!'"

The man who owned the jukebox was the first black male D.C. knew about who owned his own business, and Smith became a mentor to the young boy who was otherwise surrounded by women. D.C. learned that Smith had started off pushing a little cart and buying rags but had become a wealthy man. He had a store in Muskogee and taught D.C. many things in later years.

Aside from his excitement over the jukebox, D.C. was not always happy about the changes electricity brought to his home. "Before, we were using lamp light, and there were great long shadows in the corners of the room," he said. "I'd get over there in a booth and be real quiet and hear things I wasn't supposed to hear because they would forget I was there. With that bright light, they'd see me and say, 'Oh that boy's over there. Get out of here, sitting there with your mouth wide open. Get outa here and go to bed.'

"So I learned that everything has its positives and its negatives," he said. "They travel together." That may have been the first time D. C. made that observation. It later became a part of his philosophy about life.

Who Puts a Kid to Work at the Age of Four? Lura, That's Who

When D.C. was almost old enough to go to school, his grandmother opened a little hamburger joint. "Teenagers would come and eat hamburgers and dance to the jukebox and drink pop. My first job in the joint was as security guard," D.C. said. "On the farm, anything eatin' has to work, so they put me to work when I was four. My grandmother had a pop crate that she would sit me on in the corner of the room. She'd say, 'Now, Baby, if they start cussin' in here or making trouble, come get me. You're my eyes and ears, 'cause I'm back here in the kitchen tryin' to cook.'

13

"That was my job, and everybody knew it. So they came one night and said, 'See that little boy? Cuss real loud, say 'God damn!' Boy, I jumped off that little box and ran back saying, 'Mama, Mama! They cussin'!' When she and I came back, they all burst out laughing. She said, 'That's not funny! I know what you did. You leave that boy alone. That boy tryin' to work and ya'll messin' with 'im. I want you to leave him alone. Hear me?' Mama Lura was a strict disciplinarian, both with her own family and with her customers. She had to be, as things could get out of hand in a place where people were drinking alcohol."

"I was raised by strong women," D.C. said. "When they had to, they would jump on men in that bar. They had drawstring bags filled with perfume bottles and would use them to attack anybody who was causing trouble and beat the hell out of them. Talk about 'bag women'! They had their own meaning for that."

As an example of toughness, D.C.'s Aunt Ethel killed a white man in the bar who tried to force himself on her. He was robbing the place as Mama Lura lay dying in the front room. Ethel told the man to leave. When he didn't, she fired one shot and then said, "Get him outa here and to the doctor." She did have to go to court, but she never did any time for the killing. Eventually, word got around that the women running the place were crazy.

But for D.C., the bar was often a place for learning. "I learned to dance. I could do any dance they did," D.C. said. "My grandmother, when people would come in, would say, 'Dance for 'em.' It was kinda embarrassing, but I'd do it. They would give me quarters."

One time D.C.'s dancing brought him his first brush with fame. "My mother and father had separated at the time of my birth. In 1943, when I was eight years old, my father was in the service. He had declared me as a dependent, so we found out where he was. My mother took me to meet my dad for the first time. I'd only heard about him.

"So we got to Chicago (he was stationed at Great Lakes) and that night, we went out, the three of us. I realized then that they still loved each other, and that was a great relief to me. It was

14

some little place that had a dance contest for kids. My mother was a great dancer. She asked me if I would get in the dance contest. I said, 'Yes, if you want me to.' I got in it, and I won it. I imagine it was because I was a fat little boy trying to dance, but I did win it. So when I got back to Rentiesville, I had a certain amount of fame, because I had won a dance contest in Chicago."

Soon enough life for D.C. at the Cozy Corner went back to normal. "Well, I went on and worked. Next job I had was flipping burgers," D.C. said. "I must have been about eight then, but I had learned a lot of stuff. Mama Lura had homeschooled me until I was seven. She never bought me toys. She'd say, 'Go make yourself something to play with. Make yourself a play pretty.' Lura didn't give gifts on holidays, either. She cooked for a week and the family celebrated with food.

"I came from a line of people that taught, 'if you want something done and done right, do it yourself,'" D.C. said. "That's the attitude my grandmother had, and she taught me. She wouldn't let me start to school until a year late, when she was sure that I knew what she wanted me to know. She wanted to put her brand of formal education on me first.

"When I started to school, I could read and I could count. My grandmother made sure I got it her type of way, and I can figure in my head real good. I learned to count standing on a box making change for our customers. When I got to school, they had make-believe stores. We were told to open our cans from the bottom and bring them from home, so we could use the cans on our make-believe shelves to learn to count.

"Well, I was lightyears ahead of those kids because I had been doing the real thing in this grocery store / night club. I had been exposed to all kinds of stuff by my grandmother, and that education never did cease. All my business skills were learned from her. She got them from Doctor Clark.

"She was very excited about getting a grandson. Back in those days there was a ceiling for women, just like there is a ceiling now for women and minorities. There's just so far you're

15

going to get. But she figured an educated male could go farther in this world than an educated female.

"Now she had a male, and she was gonna, doggone it, gonna make sure this male was equipped mentally and every other possible way to make a success in this world," D C. said. "I remember in the forties when the Freedom Train came through Muskogee. It was a traveling exhibit and had the Declaration of Independence in it and had the proclamation that freed the slaves in it.

"We went up there on a snow-driven day, because she insisted that I get to see those two documents. That's how important it was to her. She was always taking me to those type things. She also taught me to wash, cook, iron, sew. She said that was so I would never have to do without. She taught me tolerance. About a drunk, she said, 'You need to go talk to him. No little boy ever wished to be a drunk when he grew up. Something happened to him along the way that threw him off his path in life. Maybe if you go talk to him when he wakes up, he'll tell you what it was that caused him to lose his way.'"

But, no matter what his grandmother did, D.C. was always drawn towards music. "In the summertime, when school was out, we'd slip into the school house," he said. "The other boys would want to go in there and play basketball in the gym. I would want to go in with them, but to play the piano. I'd be in there rockin' out, while they'd be in there playing ball. And that went on. I sang in all the operettas in school. I was in all the plays. But what I really wanted was to play guitar. That dream never died."

More than twenty years after he was sneaking into school to play piano, D.C. would go to incredible lengths to make that childhood dream of playing guitar come true. But he still had a lot to learn from his grandmother before that happened.

D. C. Got a Head Start Before There Was a Program

On Saturdays, the family would take the wagon to town to get supplies. Lura would shop and visit with her friends, but like most kids, D.C. got tired of that in a hurry. If he was good, she might let him hang out at the store that Grant Smith, the jukebox man, owned at 2nd and Dennison, just off Muskogee's Main Street.

"Upstairs in Grant Smith's place was a radio repair place; guy up there named Julius," D. C. remembered. "And right behind Grant Smith's place was an auto repair shop; guy named Dewitt. Right across the street from Grant Smith's place was Mac's. Mr. Mac had a barbeque / hamburger place then, a beer joint, with the best hamburgers I ever ate.

"I would hang out with the electronics guy upstairs, and he would explain a lot of things to me. So would the guy in the back, Dewitt. He would tell my grandmother, 'You got the smartest little boy here, such intelligent questions. He's a mannerable little boy, too, and he never gets in my way.' So he didn't mind my coming back there and hanging out. I put in my first engine when I was fourteen years old.

"I built a crystal set about that time, too. My grandmother wouldn't let me listen to the radio because, she said, 'it cost too much money to run that electric!' Julius helped me order a crystal set and helped me build it. You didn't need any batteries. All you needed were some tiny headphones, and you could hear," D.C. said. "We built a coil and the whole trip, the tuner and everything. So that was my two jump starts. I could always make my living, when the music didn't pay my way, working as a mechanic. Those gifts that I learned from those two guys at Muskogee have been with me all my life."

Early in his life, D. C. found that learning came from many sources. The confidence he had from learning about electronics when he was eight years old from Dewitt made it possible for him to learn about computers quickly when he got his first computer fifty years later.

It Took a Community to Create this Conqueror

"When you see a successful person," D.C. said when in his seventies, "there's an army of people behind him that helped get him there. What I have become is no accident." Among those people in D.C.'s life was Charlie Drennan, the Navy veteran who was a part of Lura's life from the time D.C. was a toddler until a few years before Lura died. He was the grandfather who helped Lura rear D.C.

"He would act like he was my protector," D.C. said. "He'd tell me that if I messed up, I was making his job of protecting me a lot harder. If I got into trouble with my grandma or one of my aunties or my mother, I could always run up between his knees where he was sitting and he'd throw his arms around me, tell them to leave me alone, and talk to me. When I'd do wrong, he'd say, 'we're the only men around here, and men don't act like that' or 'don't do that, that ain't right, men don't do that!'"

Drennan was a dependable supporter who also let the young boy learn some things his grandmother might not have allowed at his early age. D.C. knew how to drive a car by the age of eight. "My grandfather would let me drive his truck to the highway, which is two miles," D.C. said. "Then he would take over and drive on the highway. But one day, when I was twelve or thirteen, he said, 'Don't stop. Keep on going, Boy.' I say, 'On the highway?' He said, 'Yeah.'"

When D.C. was fourteen, the family truck was out of commission because of a bad motor and there wasn't enough money to take it to a shop for repair. D.C. heard discussion about having to wait until money was available to get a used motor installed.

"I can do it—I can put the new used motor in," D.C. declared to his grandfather.

"Are you sure? Are you sure, boy?" Drennan asked the teenager. When D.C. repeated his claim confidently, Drennan went to talk to Lura.

18

"'Now listen. I smell a messup,' was Lura's response to that big talk. But Drennan said, "Lura, you listen to me! The boy say he can do it and I believe he can."

"Next thing I knew we were up there in Muskogee at Gene Bunch's shop," D.C. remembered. "We heard the motor run in the other car, then we pulled the motor out and we got it home. I had to take the whole front end off our truck because we didn't have a hoist—we called it a 'horse.' I worked like crazy, and we got the whole thing put together again. But it wouldn't start. We knew the problem wasn't in the motor, so we got a team of horses together, hitched them to the truck and started pulling it down the road. We had six-volt batteries in those days, and it had worn down pretty fast. I got off the clutch—nothing. Over and over.

"About a mile from the house we were down by the creek and an older white neighbor I liked, old man Lane, stopped, came over and asked, 'D.C., what's wrong?' I said, 'I don't know. I put this motor in there. I know it's good...' So he said, 'Did you move this (the carburetor)?' I said no. 'Distributor?' 'Yes, I changed it.' 'Are you sure you got it in time?' I said, 'What's that?'

"Very patiently, he said, 'Let me go pull my truck off the road.' He showed me how to time it, and all about it. Charlie said, 'Boy, did you learn all that?' I did. I haven't had anybody have to teach me about timing since that day. We pulled that thing about twenty feet. I got off the clutch, and it roared to life! I turned around and drove straight to the house, with Charlie following behind with the team. Into the yard we came."

"Shit, Lura–I told you that boy could fix it!' Drennan told D.C.'s grandmother. "And a whole lot of other things around here would be better if you'd listen to me sometime!"

The House of Shame

Drennan's support was a big boost for the young boy he took under his wing. D.C. really needed people like him that he could turn to when he was young.

"People didn't want me to play with their kids because I knew too much by being in this joint," he said. "That's why I called this house 'The House of Shame.' They'd put out rumors that my grandmother was down here on this corner with three daughters and lots of drunks hanging around and that they were going to have lots of babies.

"That was a lie. There ended up just one baby here, and that was me. When I came along, they said I'd be in the penitentiary (that was McAlester) before I was eighteen years old, by my mouth or by my hand. That was the rumor mill. That was a lie, too. The only time I've been to the penitentiary was to play for those guys a few times, just like I go to nursing homes and to all kinds of other institutions, just to play music for people.

"So that's why I'm proud to say I went from a House of Shame to a Hall of Fame. What I use for that type of energy is called 'in-spite-of energy.' Don't ever let anyone tell you who you are. That's for you to determine.

"Black wasn't 'in' at the time I was growing up. People I knew were using bleaching cream to try to lighten their skin so they could get better jobs. Black Power hadn't showed itself at that time. I was double-black. I was real dark, and I was fat. And I came from a house of ill repute. If I had listened to the community and the gossip, I was doomed for failure. But I knew they were wrong, because of what my grandmother said. She said I was going to be somebody. I knew I had to get on that trail."

He never forgot the people who helped him along that trail. One of those was a very tough industrial arts teacher named Mr. Marshall who also was the basketball coach. "He realized I had a creative mind, and he wouldn't ever let me slip and slide," D.C. said. "He was a very smart man, but sensitive."

"My grandma wouldn't let me participate in sports because she was afraid I'd break my collarbone," D.C. said. "She wasn't worried about other bones, because she figured she could splint those and fix 'em, but she knew she couldn't fix a collarbone with a splint. I had to hide my sports uniforms at other kids' houses and tell my grandmother I was just going to the games. I'd walk down to the branch (creek) at the back of the field, stoop down out of sight, and then follow it over to my friend's house.

"There was a basketball tournament at Eufaula when I was in fifth grade. There were about twenty-five or thirty kids in a grade at Rentiesville when I was there. I was a little fat kid, under the protection of my grandma who wouldn't even let me take off my long underwear until such and such a date in the late spring. I didn't make the cut to go to the tournament."

"I acted like I'd been picked," he said. "I was there early that morning to be picked up to go. When we got about half way there, Mr. Marshall said, 'I've got one too many. I'll have to pay for somebody's lunch.' I didn't say anything. When we got there, I got dressed with the team. During the game, Mr. Marshall said, 'D.C., come here,' and he put me in the game. Man, I wouldn't let anybody else even see that basketball! I really played hard.

"He didn't crush me, as he could have. He knew how bad I wanted to go and knew I was still a little kid," D.C. realized. "That made him one of my favorite people ever!"

A neighbor, Mr. Duckett, was an old hobo who settled on the place as a handyman. He moved his house twice, taking it apart and rebuilding it one board at a time. He was like a great-grandfather for D.C. and tried to guide him in what it meant to be a black man. "He taught me the place of a black man. He said, 'you're not going to be driving the train, or driving a race car either. They're not going to let you do that. Don't waste your time.'"

During D.C.'s school days, Bo Jones, who was five years older than D.C. and a good musician, was another person who influenced D.C. Bo was a very popular boy and played piano well. He was a leader, mature for his age, and was good at showing other youngsters how to get things done. "He taught two of his friends, both named Sonny, to drive," D.C. remembered. "He used bed springs and an upside-down rake as a steering wheel. Both later became driving professionals, as bus drivers."

21

Bo and others in the community sometimes referred to D.C. as Deacy, or Deacyboy, as in deacon, because his grandmother insisted that he go to Sunday school and church every Sunday, even though she was not welcome at the church after she became a bootlegger. The name may have been given to D.C. because he was already a leader among his friends.

"Deacyboy, you're goin' to be a good piano player one of these days, just wait and see," Bo often told D.C. He always encouraged the younger boy to stick with music and formed a singing group that included D.C. "Not all of us were going to church regularly at that time, but we practiced a lot," D.C. said. "One Sunday all five of us showed up at church in suits and asked to be on the program. They didn't know what to make of us. But we sounded good, and they loved it. They shouted. Then we had to make the rounds and be on the music programs in all the local churches

"We were the Five Clouds of Joy. Of that group of five, three became lifetime musicians: Bo as a preacher who had his own church, Clyde LaMar who toured with the original Platters, and me."

Doris Haynes, his high school music teacher, was also instrumental in him becoming a musician. "She was a very good pianist and sang," D.C. said. "She was required as part of her teaching job to volunteer to run the choir at church, too. They would say to me, 'All your aunties and family can sing; I just know you can sing, too.' And I would get the part. Lead a lot of times, with words to memorize and all. I sang in all the musicals. They would not have it otherwise, and she (Doris) would keep me after school practicing, sharing her piano bench." The time Doris spent tutoring D.C. after school proved to be a small sacrifice in comparison to what she gave up a few years later to help him with his career.

D.C.'s Grandparents
Tom Pearson and Lura
Pearson
with their first child:
D.C's Aunt Ethel.

Grandmother Miss Lura and
Mother Helen Minner

23

Neighbor "Great-Day" with his sweet potato crop.
Miss Ewald's family just north of the Blues Club near Honey Springs.

Rentiesville Families, early 20th century.

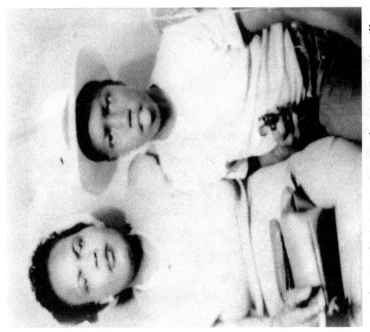
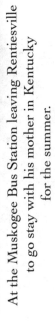

At the Muskogee Bus Station leaving Rentiesville to go stay with his mother in Kentucky for the summer.

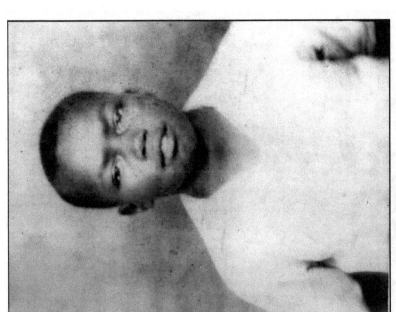

D.C. Minner, circa 1940s

JULY 1949

D.C. Minner, circa 1940s

27

Grandma Lura and D.C.; a great friendship . . . note the Hudson!

D.C. with "Baby Auntie" Elsie, his mother Helen, his Aunt Ethel, all Miss Lura's daughters, son Tony, Charlie, and Miss Lura Drennan and daughter Sheila K

"Baby Auntie" Elsie, her husband, Lodi, Miss Lura, D.C., and D.C.'s children Tony and Sheila, mid-1960's Easter Sunday.

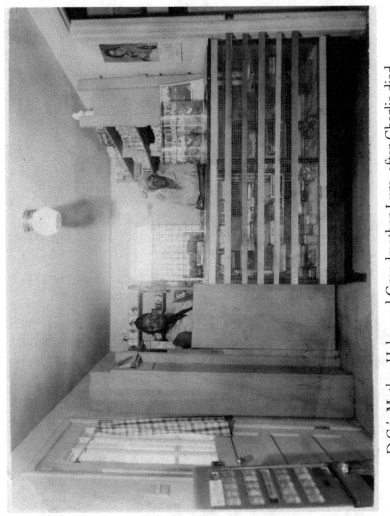

D.C.'s Mother Helen and Grandmother Lura, after Charlie died, when they were running the Grocery Store and the Cozy Corner alone in the middle 1960's.

D.C.'s beloved "Baby Auntie" Elsie and her husband Lodi Rex

An old girlfriend of D.C.'s named Billy, Charley Drennan who raised D.C. as a Grandfather, and his beloved "Mama" Lura. She said "this boy is gonna be somebody", and years later if he found himself off track, he would think about that and change his actions!

Ethel and Earl at Miss Lura's Cozy Corner

D.C.'s Aunt Ethel and Uncle Earl DeBouse, later years.

Tony Minner, Selby, D.C., Sheila
Earl, Linda, baby Erica, Ethel

D.C.'s father, Clarence Minner, meets his first great grandchild,
baby Erica Minner in Seminole OK.
His step grandaughter Sharnee on the right.

D.C. and Erica

Tony's grandson DeyDey goes to the movies
and takes a bow for the camera (below right).

Tony's daughters, the Minner sisters: Micaela, Dani, Erica first row.
Grandpa D.C., then Brandon and Selby back row.

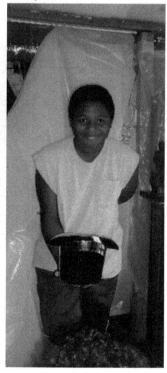

Danielle Minner
and Mom
Angela Craig
Minner Kastel

L -R Erica, D.C., Sheila K.

D.C.'s daughter
Sheila

Micaela and Dani

Dalcia Ortiz Minner and her sons Chris and Tony Minner, Jr.

Deyton, Erica and Alonzo Jackson make it to the Festival, 2004?

Erica's Darius Clark Burnett, Deyton,
Destry Burnett, & friend Mia today.

D.C.'s Grandmother Mrs. Lura Martin Pearson Drennan.
She said, "This boy is gonna be somebody!"

D.C. Minner

42

CHAPTER 2: LEAVING HOME

Lura Left Behind

Although D.C. was exceptionally close to his grandmother during childhood, the time came during his teens when he rebelled against her pushing. As a black female in the 1940's, Lura had limitations on how far her intelligence, drive, and ambition could take her. "So she was going to raise somebody that could go further," D.C. said.

"I found out that she had been grooming me all those years to be a doctor, even putting the name Doctor Clark Minner on my original birth certificate. She was the community medicine woman. She knew all the home remedies and uses of plants. She would beat up milkweed and make poultices. When anybody butchered a hog, they would hang the sex organs in a tree to save to treat mumps. In the spring she would purge me, give me her tincture to clean me out. She would rub kerosene on my navel and other things like that. And, of course, her father, who was a pharmacist, had been the community medicine man.

"I didn't want to be a doctor. So you know a teenager gets a little rebellion in 'im. My rebellious streak led me to quit school. I said, 'I'll show you. I ain't going to do what you want me to do. I'll quit school and go in the Army, and then I'll get a fair shake.' I wanted to be somewhere that I would be judged on my own merit and on that alone," D.C. remembered thinking.

"I didn't know much about segregation then because I had been raised in this black environment," he said. "I knew there was segregation within the black culture, between lighter skin and darker

43

skin. I didn't know about segregation in the world between blacks and whites. I wasn't exposed to that. Where I grew up, people were judged by their work ethic, not by the color of their skin. I might have heard whiffs of race problems from my grandmother and others here, about lynchings and things. But, firsthand, I hadn't had a chance to experience it."

He expected his grandmother to strongly object to his leaving home. D.C. had gone to Kansas City with a friend for the summer when he fifteen and had gotten a job in a foundry. "I like to starved to death," he said. "I came back on a train and started walking toward home. When she saw me, my grandmother said, 'You know, that walks like my Baby! But he's too thin to be my Baby. Ain't no place like home, is there, Baby?'"

When D.C. decided to join the military, surprisingly, Lura agreed that this might be a good thing. D.C. said he later realized she thought entering the service would be an acceptable way of moving him from her world to the outer world, while he would still have a place to stay, regular meals, and medical care. Charlie was happy because he knew, as a veteran, D.C. also would have access to health care later in life, a benefit not widely available at that time for a black man from a poor rural area.

The Military Makes the Man

"When I was in the eleventh grade, I had two buddies, Edward and James. Edward went into the service first. James and I decided we were going to go in also, on the 'buddy system,' which meant they couldn't separate us.

"They asked me, 'What do you want to do?' I said, 'I want to be a cook or a mechanic. If you'll send me to those schools, I'll join.' They said okay, they would, so I joined," D.C. remembered. "First thing they did was split James and me up, five or six days after we joined. We didn't see each other anymore."

His eight weeks of basic training were at Fort Bliss, Texas. "The next thing they did was send me to medical school to make

44

a medical technician out of me. That wasn't what I asked for, but that's the way it worked. They said my aptitude tests showed that I had that ability, so that's where I was going. I was wondering how my grandma pulled that off. I thought, 'My grandma has longer arms than even the law!'

"I guess they thought, 'He already knows something about automobiles and cooking'," D.C. said, 'So we'll teach him something brand new. But if we need him, we'll still go get him to fix our trucks'." D.C. was sent to Fort Sam Houston at San Antonio for eight weeks.

"The service taught me how the human body works," he said. "It's not unlike a car, with which I was familiar: two eyes (two headlights), an engine (a heart), fuel and exhaust. They did make a medic out of me, and then I got to go home for a visit. When I came home, I had the U.S. brass on the right side and, on the left side, I had the medical insignia, those snakes," said D.C.

"I walked in the door and my grandmother saw those snakes and said, 'Ah, a doctor! They DID make you a doctor.' I said, 'No, I'm not a doctor. I'm a medical technician.' She said, 'That's close enough thank you, Jesus!'" Later on, when other soldiers started calling him "Doc," D.C. wondered how they found out that the name on his birth certificate had been Doctor Clark Minner.

"The first time I saw the Atlantic Ocean, I crossed it!" D.C. said. "When I was assigned to go to Germany, I didn't know what that was. We used every type of transportation there was to go from San Antonio, Texas, to Bremerhaven, Germany. We rode trains, planes, helicopters, and then got on this big ship. I'd never seen one before."

When he got to Bremerhaven, the outfit he was assigned to was on maneuvers. D.C. was sent to join the outfit in the field with no equipment, no cold-weather clothing or boots, no training for cold-weather survival. His feet froze, causing circulation problems that bothered him the remainder of his life. He was never again able to wear any footwear without experiencing pain. The damage to D.C.'s feet also limited his prospects in the Army, as there were assignments he could not do. He was never required to march again and became a medic with an ambulance and a driver.

A serendipitous part of his military service was his being assigned to a four-room bunk house with three guitar players. Texan Arturo Jacobs and two other Latinos played flamenco guitar music every day. D.C. was often in the day room playing piano. "One day I said, 'Show me how to do that, man!'" D.C. remembered. "They said, 'Are you sure you want to learn how to play this kind of music?' I said, 'Yes,' and they taught me to play three songs flamenco style, as that's what they knew."

D.C. took his guitar with him the next time he went home to see his grandmother. She got excited when she saw it and asked him if he could play it. He said, "Yes, Ma'am" and sat down and played her the three songs he knew.

"She said, 'Now that you're all warmed up, play me a gospel song!'" D.C. remembered. "I said I didn't know how. She said, 'Play me some of those old blues then. I know you know how to do that!' I said, 'No, Mama. That's all I know.' She said, 'You ain't got no business carrying that guitar around and can't play nothin'!' She said she would give me a whuppin' in the morning if I didn't play her blues or a church song! Even though I was grown, I didn't want one of Mama's whuppins. So I sat up all night and figured out how to play "Precious Lord." She forced me to become a traditional musician."

Many years later, D.C. located Jacobs in Laredo, Texas, where he was working for the IRS, and told Jacobs he had become a musician. "I thanked him for getting me started on guitar," D.C. said. "He deserved to know. He was surprised and said he didn't play much anymore. His brother still played, and they would play at family picnics sometimes."

Learning to play guitar flamenco-style while in the military was an important beginning for D.C., and it got an interesting reaction from his grandmother. But he still had a dozen years to experience before his real mastery of the instrument was achieved in his mid-thirties.

"The military was like a bridge between home and the world," D.C. said. "It was like a bigger parent. I wouldn't be the man I am if I had not served in the military. It was good. I learned to take care of myself. I was sensitive enough to tune in to guys and learn from them about other ways to live. I got to see the world and got a taste of world discipline, and yet they still cared enough to make sure I got three hots and a cot. The camaraderie with other men was very important to me. That really helped me a lot. I also learned that my family was better off than I had thought. Our quality of life was rich.

"But I found there the same old cronyism, nepotism, and politics I was running away from," D.C. said. "I had joined thinking it would be a place where the best person got the best job." He was hustled by homosexual soldiers and got on the bad side of a gay superior officer who accused him of being disrespectful and made life as difficult as possible for him.

"My last days in the military were at Fort Chaffee in Arkansas," D.C. said. "I got a compassionate transfer there to be near my mother, who was in an insane asylum at Taft. She had delusions, thought she was rich. She showed up here one time with a mink stole. Her sisters said, 'You can't wear that here.' She put on that mink stole and wore it to the cemetery, in May, when it is very hot in Oklahoma. She showed them! The more they tried to talk sense to her, the more she thought they were just envious. She was paranoid. She never said a crazy thing to me, but I saw her do it to other people. She was there (in the mental hospital) six years."

D.C. had joined the military planning to stay there twenty years, but he got out in 1958 after three years, ten months, and twenty-two days. He literally grew up while in the Army. When he left Lura's home, he was 5'6" tall and weighed 145 pounds. When he returned to Oklahoma after his military service, he was 6' tall and weighed 230 pounds.

47

From Fort Chaffee to Playing Bass for Chuck Berry

While stationed in Germany, D.C. had fallen in love with a German woman, Lydia Berger, and was with her for about two years. In Oklahoma after his discharge, he told his grandmother he wanted to go back to Germany to get the woman he called Lea and bring her to Rentiesville. But Lea couldn't enter the states without a sponsor. D.C. asked his grandmother Lura to help them. She told him that, if he still wanted to go in six months, she would give him the money to go and would act as Lea's sponsor.

"My grandmother knew me pretty well," D.C. said. "And she wanted her grandchildren to grow up here in Rentiesville. When I got home from the service, Doris, my music teacher from high school was here with my grandmother to greet me. She said, 'Look what the army did for me!' Doris Haynes, who had tutored D.C. after school before he left for the military, was also a good friend of Lura's and had spent a lot of time with her while D.C. was out of the country. It wasn't long before D.C. and Doris started dating.

I was twenty-two and she was twenty-nine, with a five-year-old son, Relfus, called "BoBo." We were the talk of the town," D.C. remembered. "One month later, we were married!" Lura got her way, and her grandchildren would be reared in Rentiesville.

"Doris was a very good pianist and sang as well. She ran the choir at church, as well as teaching music. So when I married her, I married her music, too. Subliminally, somewhere back in there, you know, thinking maybe it would rub off, like magic, magically transfer to me. She could read music and said I was not a real musician because I couldn't read music. My friends and I played by ear, in the African oral tradition," D.C. said. "I would flip the light switch off so that she couldn't see her music – of course she had to stop playing and then tell her, 'A real musician can still play with the light out!'

"She wouldn't let me play her piano—she said the music I wanted to play would 'knock it out of tune,' which was completely untrue, of course. But otherwise, Doris always supported my music and never wanted to hold me back. We never, never fell out."

With the training and experience he'd had in the military, D.C. got a job as a medical technician at the Veteran's Administration Hospital in Oklahoma City. Doris and her son, Bobo, stayed in Rentiesville where she was teaching music. Soon D.C.'s and Doris' first child, Tony, was born.

D.C.'s job brought him in contact with a musician who would provide an opportunity for D.C. to pursue his interest in music. "There was a guy named Johnny B. Ellis who worked in the kitchen at the place where I worked," D.C. recalled. "He delivered special diet milkshakes and other things around the hospital. He would always come in looking tired and told me he played in a band with his wife, Miss Blues. I told him I played guitar, and he said, 'Bring it with you and come to where we're playing sometime.' I said, 'Okay.'

"The band was playing on Saturday night. I can still hear that band. I could hear them in the parking lot when I went out there, off NE 23rd in Oklahoma City. That first night I didn't attempt to play. I had my guitar with me, but I thought it might be broke because it didn't sound right when I played it. I wasn't sure it would really play music, so I let Little Eddie (a band member) play it just to hear it. He said, 'It's a good one, man!' It was. I had a Gibson.

"Next day was Sunday, and they had a gig in the afternoon, so I went," D.C. said. 'Why don't you come up and play one, man,' Eddie asked me. So I got up and played my little bass line on the guitar: boom boom boom boom...boom boom booom booom. So I kept going back and sitting in. Their regular bass player preferred to play Delta blues, a different style from what this group was doing. He really just wanted to hunt and fish on weekends, instead of playing with that band. That was a stroke of luck for me. They asked me to play bass with them, which was my first experience playing music with a group.

"One day Eddie said to me, 'You know, they make a special guitar just for that (playing the bass line).' 'No, really?' I said. 'Yeah, they call it a bass—you need to get one,' he said. I had the good government job, so I had credit. He took me to the music store. The electric bass was so new (in 1959) that they didn't have one in the store. The man showed me one in a book and said he would have it come in on a bus from Tulsa, and it would be in tomorrow." D.C. got a loan from his very thrifty grandmother Lura, which took some good talking to accomplish, and bought the bass. At first he could only play that one pattern and only in one key. D.C. played the bass with a capo (a type of clamp), normally used only on a guitar.

"People made fun of me," he said. "Them ol' boys laughin' at me made me determined to stop their laughing." With Doris, Tony, and "Bobo" in Rentiesville, D.C. concentrated on improving his skills as a musician. "I would come home from a gig, set up my bass and go over every tune again, particularly the ones I'd had trouble with. Three o'clock in the morning I was sitting in my motel room practicing, practicing," D.C. said. "Practice, hard work, and determination. It works every time. I call it the Powerful P's: Proper Preparation Prevents Piss Poor Performance! After a while the word was out that I was the best bass player in town. The very people who had laughed at me came back and clapped for me—and hired me!"

Soon he went to work with the best group in town, Larry Johnson and the New Breed, which was the house band at the Bryant Center. Later he started putting bands together and getting the bookings. It wasn't long before band leaders of established groups came looking for him. One of those was the "Godfather of Soul," singer and dancer James Brown.

"That certainly had the neighborhood down on 9th Street talking," he remembered. He then had numerous opportunities to tour with bands who had hit records. But while his career as a musician thrived, his marriage and his health weren't doing as well.

His work at the VA hospital so stressed and exhausted D.C. that he was not a pleasant person to be around when he was home with his family. The suffering he saw and his deep compassion for the problems of the men he served daily left him with less patience and attention for his wife and children than they had reason to expect from him.

"I was too sensitive to the problems of the patients and too insensitive to my family," he said. "One time I ran over the family dog and wasn't sensitive to the family's grief. My wife really told me off then. Doris wouldn't let me grow up," D.C. said. "I was always a boy to her."

D.C.'s daughter, Sheila, was born while Doris, "Bobo", and Tony were still living in Rentiesville. Rearing three children, mostly by herself, while D.C. worked and played music elsewhere, took its toll on Doris, as well as on D.C. The couple fought over Doris' heavy drinking, as well as over their diverging lifestyles. After several stormy years, the couple split up for good in 1965.

"She had wanted the divorce," D.C. said. "We went down and signed the papers and then went home and went to bed together. But we never, never fell out. I've been blessed with good women in my life. Doris was one of them. When I was put in the Oklahoma Music Hall of Fame, I publicly thanked my first wife (Doris), as well as my wife Selby.

"I realized, years after it happened, that Doris had given me my freedom so that I could pursue a musical career. She had sacrificed a professional career in music to be a parent, and she could see that I would do the same thing, as I was missing opportunities to tour because of my VA job. She had some of her friends in Oklahoma City check on me. They told her I was gifted. She kicked me out so that I could become all I was capable of being."

Doris had a very bad auto accident after the couple split up and broke bones in her face. Her doctor told her she must quit drinking because the blood vessels in her head couldn't stand it if her blood pressure rose. However, Doris was unable to stop drinking. She had a stroke and died soon afterward in 1968.

After Doris's death, her great-aunt Altonia Morris Ferguson Nutter, who had raised Doris, took over and raised Doris and D.C.'s children. Sister, as she was called by the family, was the town clerk, the principal of the Rentiesville school and a very strong, forceful woman. As has been the case with some other black women in the past (including Lura), Sister valued male children over females. She doted on Sheila's brother Tony, leaving his little sister feeling lonely and unwanted. Years later, Selby said of this show of favoritism, "Maybe even more than Doris, D.C.'s daughter Sheila paid a price for D.C.'s career. Sheila was 'daddy's girl' and was devastated by being separated from her father."

The wounds D.C.'s children suffered from their parents' breakup and from Doris's death while they were still young affected both Sheila and Tony on into their later lives.

I've been lost and confused
and didn't know which way to go.
(from "Blues for Bobo," D.C. Minner)

If Doris divorced D.C. to give him the opportunity to "be all he could be," as D.C. later believed she had done, she may have been disappointed by the short-term result of her sacrifice. What D.C. became, for a time in the mid-sixties, was a spoiled, self-indulgent substance abuser, very streetwise, living with and off of women who sought him out and turned him on to the fast life after he began to succeed as a musician.

"When I was a little boy, I was so black I was blue. They used to call me blue. My best friend was Eugene, because he was as black as me. I was fat and I was black. I didn't have none of the qualities of the 'beautiful people.' That was long before James Brown came up with 'Say it loud and say it proud: black is beautiful.' In Oklahoma City, I discovered 'bennies' (amphetamines) and lost weight. Then black power came along and black was 'in'," he said. "All of a sudden, I was cool. I had missed out on that earlier because I was fat and not an athlete. My bass playing had got good. I was invited to parties and treated like I was light and cute. The girls found me. I'd never before had so much attention," he said.

As did the other musicians he worked and traveled with, D.C. sometimes lived with high-class prostitutes. One who often brought in as much as a thousand dollars a day introduced him to hard drugs. She would also send him out to buy, with money she earned, jewelry and clothing for himself. D.C. fell into the fast life of a successful musician with the same intensity he brought to everything he did.

After six or seven years in Oklahoma City, D.C. was respected as one of Oklahoma's best bass players. He was scouted by well-known musicians like James Brown and never went without work. He played bass with Little Miss Peggy and James Walker. He played behind Chuck Berry, O.V. Wright, Eddie Floyd (of "Knock on Wood" fame), and Bo Diddley, among others. Blues great Freddie King found him and took him on tour with him for two years.

"I impressed Grant Smith (the entrepreneur from his childhood who went from being a rag man to being the wealthiest black man in Muskogee) when I played with Freddie King," D.C. remembered. "I took Mama (Lura) to see me play with Freddie. She said, 'Tell him to come over here.' Freddie went to talk to her. She shook his hand and said, 'There are a few things I want to go over with you. Why don't you let this boy sing? And you shouldn't make him stand up there so long–that's too long. King said, 'Yes, ma'am, you're right. Glad to meet you.' D.C. later apologized to Freddie, and his response was, "Shoosh, man, I got a grandma too!"

"That was the beginning of a great friendship with King," D.C. said. "When he came to Oklahoma City, he stayed with me. He was quite a character. He weighed 340 pounds and I weighed 265. We were like a matched set of bookends on stage. We could communicate without any words. Freddie learned to play from his momma. What your momma teaches you goes in deeper, because you trust her. Freddie started out with a cigar box guitar and reached the heights he did," D.C. said.

The New Breed Band did weekly gigs in both Oklahoma City and Wichita for years. They were based in Memphis for a couple of years as the backup band for O.V. Wright and toured across the South and played as far north as Boston behind Wright, with great success and big audiences.

"I got so busy, still running the band all that time, that I never rested," he said. "Finally that made me sick." The fast life was taking its toll on him. By the late sixties, he had been hospitalized with cirrhosis of the liver, jaundice, and hepatitis which he had all at the same time.

"Doing drugs and chasing girls caused it," D.C. said in his later years. "It was alcohol and lack of rest. The whores took all the energy out of me. I never once went looking for a whore, though. They found me.

"But whores freed me from materialism," he said. "They gave me everything a black man thinks he wants: sex, Cadillacs, diamonds, houses. I had everything money could buy, and I was still unhappy. I learned that money was not the answer to everything. Most people don't get the chance to learn that early enough in their lives." D.C. woke up to his situation after five years of keeping the company of a beautiful, long-legged blonde prostitute from Houston.

"She said to me, 'Boogie, you know why I have you?' I said I thought I had her. She said, 'No, I saw your little country-boy ass comin' a long way off. I take money from men, take food out of their families' mouths! I keep you around because when I wake up in the morning, I need to look at somebody who is sorrier than I am. That's what you do for me, Boogie! That's your job.'" That remark was a wakeup call. Suddenly obvious to D.C. was that the life he was living at that time was not the one Doris and his grandmother had prepare him for through their sacrifices.

"When I left her (the blonde prostitute), I changed my values," he said. "I wanted out of the fast lane, and she didn't. I got one room and switched from bass to guitar." He set out on a different path, one that would get him back on the road to becoming the man his grandmother Lura had expected him to be.

D.C. wins a sharp shooter game in Germany while in the service

D.C. in Germany in the Army third from left. He was a medic.

Above: D.C. on right as a beginning bassist in Johnny B. Ellis
(keyboard) and Dorothy Ellis' (Miss Blues) band
in Oklahoma City in the 50's.

Below: friend Little Miss Peggy worked with Bill Parker and
the Showboat Band: moved to OKC from New Orleans.

Larry Johnson and the New Breed out of OKC, house band at the Bryant Center for many years. This is the band which toured with Freddie King and OV Wright off and on for two years each.

They also performed on the show with BB King in Memphis and toured with Eddie Floyd while he had the hit song "Knock On Wood," with Chuck Berry, Bo Diddley and many more. The band moved to Denver for a while and played a club at Five Points. Several including Larry Johnson eventually settled in California where they continued to perform. Not in the photo is Tank Jernigan who later worked for Capitol Records in Hollywood, creating horn charts for many of Ray Charles' records.

L - R Larry Johnson, Vernon Powers, Madd Ladd, and D.C. on the right (late 50's)

D. C. and his bass guitar in OKC

Doris Morris Haynes Minner with her first child Relfus J. Haynes. D.C. Minner's first wife, mother of his children Sheila K Minner and Tony Minner, Singer, pianist and teacher. She was very supportive of his music career.

D.C. Minner

60

D.C. Minner

CHAPTER 3: DISCOVERING CALIFORNIA

If I don't know where I'm goin',
Any road will get me there.
(from "Blues for Bobo," D.C.Minner)

After ten years spent touring and living in Memphis, Denver, Wichita, Colorado Springs, and Oklahoma City, the New Breed Band broke up. D.C. and guitarist Larry Johnson headed for Los Angeles in 1969, following several musician friends who were working and doing well there. Among D.C.'s contacts in California were Tony Mathews from Checotah, Claude Williams, and Melvin "Tank" Jernigan, who had all played with him in the New Breed Band in Oklahoma City.

The scene they ran into when they moved to LA in the late sixties was documented in the Ray Charles movie, *Ray*. Dr. George Carney said in an article, "Red Dirt and Blues," that "Tony Mathews actually toured the world with Ray for eighteen years as his guitarist. Tony also worked with Little Richard for two years. Claude Williams played trumpet for Ike and Tina Turner. Melvin 'Tank' Jernigan became horn arranger for Capitol Records, working on many of Ray Charles' recordings. He also played the flute part on (Canned Heat's) "Goin to the Country," which was a monster hit, later featured on a national television ad for Volkswagen."

Tony was a few years younger than D.C. and had the opportunity to study guitar under Tim Guilkey, an Oklahoman who was a master at Delta-style guitar playing. Guilkey left

Oklahoma to live in Kansas and was not around for more than two or three days at a time while D.C. was growing up. "When he would come home to see his mom, he'd end up down here with his electric guitar and his amplifier," D.C. said. "He would sit in our kitchen and play. I would just sit there in awe and watch him and wish he lived here, so I could get him to show me how to do it. Tim moved back here after I was in the service and Tony started taking lessons from him, which was an opportunity I'd missed. Tony sings about Tim and Rentiesville on his Alligator Records release "Condition Blue." Tony went on to become one of the best guitar players on the planet."

D.C. met up with Mathews again in Los Angeles in 1969 and was quickly recruited to play bass in the Ton Ton Macoute band in a club on Sunset Boulevard in Hollywood called Citadel De Haiti. The club was owned at that time by Bernie Hamilton, the actor who played the black police officer in "Starsky and Hutch."

A Life-Changing Event

Gene Edwards, a professional jazz guitarist, was a recording artist in town. He walked up to Tony and D.C. in Hollywood and said, "Hello, Scorpio; Hello, Aquarius," and started talking to them about their lives and their beliefs. They were both amazed. How did this man they had never seen or spoken to before know so much about them?

"Gene really pulled my coat," D.C. said. "He said, 'That stuff you are thinking and talking about—there's a study for that. All that stuff you are complaining about—the answer to it is here in these books.' I was still asleep at that time. I didn't know the power I had. I did think, though, it was time I got out of bed and invested my time better."

Both D.C. and Tony began studying Yogananda's book *The Autobiography of a Yogi*, which is one of the most revealing books of the spiritual wealth of India ever to be published in the West. Focusing on the science of spiritual exploration, Yogananda's mission was "'Yoga for the West." In hundreds of American cities, he taught the largest yoga classes in the world. Tony and D.C. worked with Gene, whom they called their guru, for three years. They also studied numerology and astrology. "He was an amazing man," D.C. said of Edwards. "He was trying to free the world from materialism, fear, superstition and violence. He said it was his job to get people to re-channel violence, and that he had gotten a very violent man to take his violence out on a chessboard. He told us to study, listen, and then go out and try to prove these books a lie. If you do, he told us, throw them away. We were looking for the essence of our being. I still have the books."

Edwards worked to persuade others that money was not really as important as many people seemed to think. D.C. had already started moving away from materialism and was ready to soak up Edwards' lessons. "I had been thinking yoga, really, without knowing what it was, all my life," he said. "My grandmother was a very disciplined woman. She was a Capricorn and a Capricorn believes in order. She taught me discipline and raised me not to go along with the crowd, but to be an independent thinker. She knew she couldn't make me succeed, but she had the vision to make me feel that way on the inside. What she was doing was programming me, and it worked. I called myself rebelling against her obvious programming, but there was a deeper layer I didn't know about."

Thinking he was retiring from being a performer, D.C. went back to Oklahoma in the late sixties, planning to help his grandmother run the Cozy Corner. He started by building some gogo stands for dancers and painting the place purple. But his grandmother had been managing all those years without him and had her own ideas about how things should be done. "Well, her friends, local cowboys, were starting all the trouble in there, and I'd kick them out," he remembered. "'You can't kick him out! He's my friend,' she'd say. She finally got down to the point. She said, 'You know what, Baby. You're young; you can go any place in this world and make it. I'm an old woman; I can't go nowhere but right here. One of us is going to have to leave!'"

D.C. laughingly recalled that his mother and grandmother had burned his astrology books while he was in Oklahoma. "I was wearing dreds, the Jamaican hairstyle later popularized by reggae artists. They thought I had gone off the deep end," he said. "But they still planted by the moon and used herbs to treat sickness."

D.C. returned to California for more years of studying philosophy under the guidance of Gene Edwards. "I studied really hard because I wanted to prove that my grandmother was right about me 'being somebody' and that all those people who said I'd end up in a penitentiary were wrong. I started looking at myself and dealing with who I was, rather than who I wished I was.

"Everybody has three people: who 'they is,' who 'they think they is', and 'who they want to be'. I had to move into who I was and start coming from that aspect. Once I did that, and found out a lot things about myself and that I could do whatever I wanted to do, that was a turning point in my life."

California Suited His Style

"After seeing something of the world, I realized at some point that there must be a better way than I knew about. Low self-esteem caused me to mistreat people when I was younger. I mistreated myself even worse than I mistreated others. I asked God to forgive me. Then I checked out all the religions I could find. Some of them had one thing I didn't believe in: that is, that there is only one way. 'If you don't do this the way I've done it,' they might tell you, 'you are not gonna be saved.'

"I couldn't see a just God letting all the rest of the people in the world go, just because they didn't have this one belief. And when I got to studying yoga and the occult, I found the answers I had been looking for. The message in all those groups (religions), the main message they all came here to teach, is that there is life after death. You may have thirty contradicting versions over there on the other side, when you run your plan to build a church, but you all have to believe in the hereafter. Jesus was

66

very successful in freeing man from thinking there is only one way. And they all teach 'do unto others.'

"The hereafter is all about karma. It's saying, 'What you do over here is going to affect your life every day, as well as your situation when you get over there.' That's what Jesus meant when he said, 'Do unto others' and 'Turn the other cheek.' Then it's on the other guy! It's definitely on him, for sure. The first time a dog bites you, it could be an accident. It ain't your fault. But, definitely, if that same dog bites you again, it can't be nobody's fault but yours, because by then you do know the dog will bite!

"If you have an experience and you don't gain any knowledge from it, it's a waste. There is no mistake, as long as you learn from it. It may be a costly lesson, but it's not a mistake, if you learn. It's only a mistake if you go through it, pay for it and don't learn anything. Then you've got a problem. That's a negative, and it's subject to happen again and again, until you come out of denial.

"I got free when I was thirty-five," he said. "That girl who called me Boogie couldn't stand for anybody to have more jewelry or a better car than I had. My Cadillac was my pride and joy when I was in Oklahoma City. It was pink, after all, with the huge fins. When I got to Hollywood, everybody there was driving foreign cars: Lamborghinis, Ferraris and Jaguars.

"I found myself parking a couple of blocks away and walking to the party so no one would know what I was driving. I began to realize that there is no end in sight to the acquisition of wealth and the tokens of status. I had gone from being a big fish in a small pond to being a little fish in a big pond, and it was clear there were ever bigger ponds over the horizon. I found I had been reacting to the world, instead of acting. When you are reacting, somebody else is calling the shots. Acting, you are starting the action in motion. Reacting, I was always behind the eight ball. I needed to take control."

And take control he did. Looking for time to study, he moved north. In addition to friends, D.C. had family in California. His father, Clarence, D.C.'s stepmother Willie, and their family were living in Stockton at that time.

D.C. got to know his father for the first time when he went to California in 1968. He found his father's address in a phone book and went to see him. D.C. said that, as soon as he saw his father and talked to him, the anger that D.C. had felt because his father had not been a part of his life in Oklahoma all went away.

"My father was what was known in Oklahoma as an Uppity Negro," D.C. said. "California was where he needed to be."

D.C. complained to friends that people in Los Angeles weren't very friendly. "They could be next-door neighbors for years and not even speak to each other," D.C. pointed out to his friend. The friend replied, "You know, D, northern California would suit you better."

"So I went up to visit my stepsister in Berkeley," D.C. said. "We were riding down Telegraph Avenue. My stepmother, Willie Minner, said, 'You ain't never seen nothing like this! Just look at them!'

"I was looking out there and saw all those freaks," D.C. remembered. "I said 'Jesus, these are my people!' I was thinking, 'Stop the car!' That was where I wanted to be. I couldn't wait to get out there. As soon as they got me to her daughter's house, I said I had to go out for some cigarettes. I went out and mixed with the hippies and bought me a joint. I loved Berkeley. I had the same political thing as the hippies did. I went Rastafarian. My family said, 'Oh, my God—comb your hair!'

"I moved up to the Bay area and pretty much did a hermit trip there on my own, right in the middle of the city," D.C. said. "From L.A. to the woods was a gradual process of withdrawing farther and farther into myself. I didn't have time for girlfriends. That was part of the thing I left behind me in L.A. I wanted to leave that life style, the cars, the fast living, behind, too.

"I moved into an old hot dog stand just off Telegraph, south of the Berkeley / Oakland city line," he said. "I did astrological charts and got people to buy me a book occasionally in exchange for doing their charts. I did a lot of reading and a lot of studying.

I started really looking at myself. I found out a lot of things about myself, and that I could do whatever I wanted to do. It was a turning point."

With what D.C. had learned early in life, he had no problem supporting himself with odd jobs, some odder than others. After a friend gave him an old sewing machine, Lura's grandson used it to make fancy women's clothing, which he sold very successfully on Telegraph Avenue. The sight of a large, wild-looking black man selling dainty feminine garments on the street got a lot of attention. He would then tell them, "I know what men like. I know how to make you look good!"

But after more than three years of studying, thinking and refining his beliefs, D.C. decided the time had come to challenge himself to do something with his recently-found knowledge.

Testing the Discipline

"After that came the time for a test," D.C. said. "I had to find out if I was really, really in control of myself. The test was a discipline. Who's in charge? Everybody should ask himself that question: 'Who's doing who?' Because you have to learn to say 'no' to yourself. 'No' 'Yeah, but I want that.' 'No!'

"Once I finished studying, I had to sacrifice. It's only a sacrifice when it means giving up something you really cherish. So I chose talking, sound. Sound has always been special to me. I love to talk. I love to sing. I love to play music. So I gave up speaking. It would have been easier for me to give up eating. In 1972, I did a verbal fast for seven months and sixteen days. No sound. I didn't laugh. I didn't make any sound. I communicated only with a clipboard. I have all those notes from that time under my bed today (in 2007). It taught me how to listen. I learned a lot about people. I walked the streets all day, meeting new people."

D.C. recalls that during the verbal fast, he had to see a dentist. When he went back to the dentist after ending the fast, the dentist said, "It's a miracle! You've learned to talk!" After D.C. explained his reason for not talking, the dentist said, "I've always wanted to stop talking, but I owe too much money to be able to do it!"

"The day came when I had to choose whether to break the fast or to stay on it for the rest of my life, as it was very comfortable to me," D.C. said. "There was an imaginary pool of water in my mind that was perfectly calm. I was afraid if I started talking, it would become turbulent. That was one of the things going on with me, but that was all selfish.

"I got to thinking that I had children that I had brought into the world and had encouraged, enticed, them to love me. And here I was in nirvana, sitting on top of a mountain in a state of bliss, but not taking care of my responsibilities that I had previously obligated myself to. In order to really deal with that, I had to come back to the world. So I broke the fast with a prayer.

"I couldn't be what I am now if I had continued that. I would have felt good, but that was just me. I wouldn't have made other people feel good. But that fast was a major, major step. After that, I knew I could do anything I wanted to do," he said.

Where Do I Go From Here?

> I packed up and quit my job.
> Say I quit my job, Baby,
> and packed up everything I own . . .
> (From "Blues for Bobo," D.C. Minner)

"After I broke the verbal fast, I had to decide, right away, what I wanted to do with my life," D.C. said. "I was in my thirties. I took an accounting of my skills and asked myself, 'What do I really want?' It all boiled down to how much of my time I was willing to invest in whatever project I got myself involved in. It's just that simple. Humans learn by a process of trial and elimination. If you try enough things and eliminate enough things, the obvious answer is left.

"So, anyway, I thought about going back to school. Since I had all this information and was as powerful as I wanted to be in determining my destiny, what was I going to do? The first thing that popped up was my Grandma Lura. She wanted me to become a doctor, so maybe that's what I should do. It would be a huge project. Trying to be a doctor would be making that maximum effort for a goal somebody else wanted. That was too much work to do for somebody else.

"I had always wanted to play guitar well and sing and be the front man for the band, instead of the bass player. To learn to do that would also be a very difficult job. One difference: I *wanted* to be a front man. I started taking inventory of my experiences. Oh, you've been a mechanic, you've done this and you've done that. But most of all, it came out that I had been a musician for nineteen or twenty years. I loved music and had a lot of experience there, but I'd never really gotten to the front of the band where I wanted to be, singing and playing that guitar."

"Maybe I could do that now. Maybe I will do that now. So, oh, yeah! I can capitalize on what I've already learned. I had been to the mountain top as a bass player but now I wanted to be up front," he said. "So, instead of hanging on to the ankles down there, somewhere, I decided to go for the throat! I knew what I wanted. I wanted to stand up in front and wink at the girls! To do that, I had to prepare myself. I picked up that guitar again.

"By that time, I'd played bass behind some of the best guitar players in the world: Freddie King, Chuck Berry, Larry Johnson, and Bo Diddley. I knew what I had to do. To accomplish it, I realized I would have to go into isolation, because I wasn't going to find anybody else immediately that had the kind of conviction I had at that time. Everyone who learns to play an instrument has a certain number of bad notes they have to play before they get to the good ones, and it was something I had to do alone. When you get an idea and find you are more serious than the people around you, you can't let them pull you off your track.

"Also, Yogananda teaches that solitude is needed to become established in the self, with a later return to the world, to serve it," D.C. said. "Yogananda students are taught, after they return from solitude, to then strive selflessly to inspire and uplift fellow humans.

"So I started asking people where I could find an isolated spot where I would not be disturbed. Some of my hippie friends took me to a spot in the north redwoods in rural Humboldt County and showed me a spot on government land west of White Thorn on the Lost Coast, five miles from any other human being."

"I could hear the ocean, half a mile away. The verbal fast had been broken two or three months by then. I was on the trail," he said. "I got there in October, which was when everybody else was leaving, because it rains there every day in the winter.

"I took twenty-five pounds of rice, twenty-five pounds of beans and a nylon-string guitar. I built a little room about 8'x8', I guess. I wrapped that building up in black plastic. I took a big roll of plastic and just went around and around it and cut my door out. Across the top, I stretched chicken wire and put clear plastic so I could have some light. I had a step van, so I went to the Berkeley dump and furnished my living quarters.

"I was racing the weather, trying to get a shelter so I could stay dry and warm. I spent about a month going to the Berkeley dump every day collecting things in order to do this. I got a lot of stuff out of there. Sometimes I'd have to give the guy there a dollar for something really good, to keep him from totally losing out. It was hard for him to watch me down there, you know. He could have run me out of there and said, 'Hey you can't do that!' But he knew we were looking for different stuff. I was looking for an old cook stove and straight boards, a cot, that kind of thing.

"I couldn't drive all the way up to my house. I had to walk in the last two miles carrying what I needed," he said. "That's called the Lost Coast up there, in rural Humboldt County. I spent a lot of time and effort, trying to get away from people. I knew what I wanted. The question was, how much was I willing to invest? I put it all in, gave it my all. I was totally isolated.

72

"I would boil the rice, play my guitar, eat rice, play my guitar, boil the beans, play my guitar, eat beans, play guitar, eat rice and beans, play my guitar and do it all over again. I knew what the music was supposed to sound like, from playing with great guitar players. I knew when I got it right and I knew when I got it wrong. If I had to go to the city for supplies, I would see my friends, who would tell me I was missing out on all the fun and all the girls. I told them, after I learned to play that guitar, I'd have all the girls I wanted. I said if they knew what I knew, they'd be up in those woods, too.

"People now say to me, 'You're so lucky! You know how to play the guitar!' That's not luck," D.C. commented in later years. "That's a result of hard work and determination. If any luck was involved, it's that I was fortunate enough to discover that I had the discipline within myself to stay focused and apply myself.

"Every human being that picks up an instrument has a certain amount of bad notes they have to play before they can hear the good notes they want to play, because the music wants to know: 'are you listening?' It's like open pit mining. They take rock off the top before they get to the good stuff. They may move trash rock for something like 20 years before they get any precious stuff out of it. In the process, they get everything out of there. You have to play a certain number of bad notes before you get to the good stuff, just like on that mountain. If they took one truck load off that mountain every day, it would take much longer than if they carried away one hundred loads a day or a thousand loads a day. That's why I isolated myself.

"So, the more you play, the faster you get to the good notes you want to hear," D.C. said. "I have to play this guitar until the notes are as beautiful as I can make them. That's my goal. I promised to do that. That's why I was entrusted with the talent."

After seven months of near-solitude, D.C. had written twenty-six songs and was ready to try them out on an audience.

Looking for a Lab

Going back down to the Bay area a few months later was another turning point," D.C. said. "I needed an audience to tell me if my songs were songs. I'd never even been in a coffee house in my life. I didn't know nothing about 'em. But I needed a lab, a workshop. Every artist does. Those hootenanny-type things were good for that. I needed to get back to the city, back on the trail.

"There were a lot of kids down there. They had one set of dreams, and I had a whole other set of dreams. I was working on a gig to go to Japan. Most of those kids playing there were on their way up for the first time. I had been to the top of the pile as a bass player, and now I was trying to get on my way to make it to the top again. I was just like most students that are older than their peer group. I was much more serious because I knew what I was aiming for. I wasn't aiming in the dark. You pay your dues and move up to the next stage.

"My next stage was being the front man. With that position goes a lot of responsibility. When I was playing bass, if the show was a failure, it wasn't my fault. If the audience didn't like it, it was because of the front man. What I wanted to learn at the coffee houses was whether people would clap when I played guitar and sang the songs I had written," D.C. said. "If all of a sudden everybody had got up to go to the bathroom at the same time, or if they all went outside together, that would make you feel funny. But that didn't happen."

While playing nights at the coffee houses, D.C. opened a garage and had such a successful mechanic's business that it almost kept him from pursuing his career in music. But, as fate would have it, D.C. was destined to follow that career and to experience a few surprises in his personal life.

Women Teaching D.C. "What For"

Generally D.C. got along very well with women, having been reared in a house full of them and loving women as he did. He often poked fun at himself for some of the situations he got himself into. When D.C's. friends kidded him about missing out

74

on the great parties in Berkeley while he was in rural Humboldt County, he told them he would have all the girl friends he wanted after he learned to play his guitar well. And so he did.

During the time he was isolated on the northern California coast learning to play lead guitar, he was interrupted one day by an old girlfriend who had gotten so angry with him for his self-chosen isolation that she drove as far as the terrain allowed, then she walked the rest of the way in so she could tell him off. "I couldn't believe it!" he said. "I said to her, 'You came all the way up here just so you could yell at me?'"

He also did a thorough job of upsetting an Italian woman he was living with after his time in seclusion. "She was a little bitty woman, but she was a martial arts expert," D.C. said. "She had a really bad temper. She would go to garage sales and flea markets just to buy cheap dishes to throw at me! I decided I was goin' to leave her. When she saw me with my suitcase, she got between me and the door and drew herself up into her martial arts stance and hissed at me! She wouldn't let me out the door.

"I finally called the cops and said I was wanting to leave and the woman wouldn't let me go. When the cop got there, he looked at me—I was six feet tall and 230 pounds and he looked at her. He was incredulous that I had called for help, as I was twice her size. Then she went into her martial arts routine at him, and that big tough cop unsnapped his holster and called for some backup! The second cop came. Seeing there were finally enough big strong men on hand to deal with her, she was just as sweet and reasonable as she could be. The second cop was greatly put out that we'd called him. The first cop was stammerin' and stutterin' and sayin' 'You just had to be here! She was really . . .'"

"I was really chasing women when I lived in Berkeley," he said. "One night a white girl picked me up in a club. When we got to her house, we got in bed. But then she said, 'I just can't do this.' 'What do you mean—you can't do it?' I demanded. She said, 'I just can't take advantage of you like this.' 'Take advantage of me?' I asked. 'The only reason I brought you here is because it's politically correct,' she said, "and it's not fair for me to use you like that.' I said, 'Oh, go ahead, girl. Just use me 'til you use me up!'"

Before he got together with Selby, D.C. had five girlfriends all at the same time. The women knew each other, and through their talk, they all knew D.C. was flitting around among them pretty much as he pleased. "One of them invited me to dinner, and when I arrived, they were all in there. They had been there some time. I said 'Excuse me I have to go buy some cigarettes,' and they said 'No, we already have your cigarettes, come in.' They then proceeded to tell on me one after the other, 'first he says this,' 'then he says that,' and I finally said 'I guess you are all tired of me now and I will just go.' They responded 'No, we still like you but we are going to change the rules of the game. We are in charge now,' and that I would come and go when they told me to come and go.

"That lasted a while, but it took a lot of the fun out of the situation; I learned just how it felt to be used."

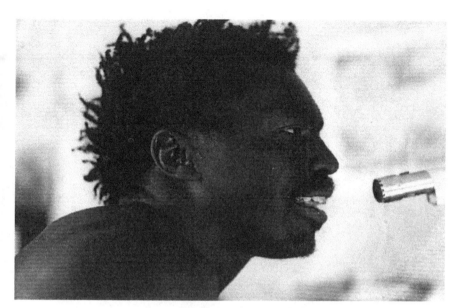

Recording himself in Berkeley

D.C. During the time of self discovery while living
in the redwoods of Humboldt County circa 1975

D.C. At a recording session at Ike Turner's studio in Los Angeles.

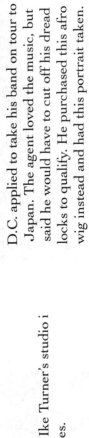

D.C. applied to take his band on tour to Japan. The agent loved the music, but said he would have to cut off his dread locks to qualify. He purchased this afro wig instead and had this portrait taken. The agent was very pleased!

Larry Johnson (upper left) and the New Breed. (mid 60's) D.C. was the bassist, upper right. This was taken in Hollywood.

California suited his style.

Fishing with Bob and his cane pole.

Larry Johnson (upper left) and the New Breed. (mid 1960's)
D.C. was the bassist, upper right.
This was taken in Hollywood.

CHAPTER 4: SELBY & D.C.

Was It Love at First Sight?

Love is a dream, a beautiful dream for two
When you find the right one to make
your dream come true
Life isn't real until your heart can feel
The bliss of a sweet romantic kiss
and the joys I promise you'll never miss.
(From "Lover's Dream" by D.C. Minner)

As a youngster, D.C. would sometimes gaze up at the moon. When his grandmother Lura caught him doing it, she would say, "There is somebody for every one of us. Your somebody is looking at the same moon you are looking at. You'll find her, Baby." It didn't happen quickly for D.C., but it did happen.

D.C. spotted Selby soon after she arrived in Berkeley with another man, Jim Donovan, in 1971. "We were walking with our guitars on our backs in gig bags," Selby said. "We were getting ready to catch a bus and go investigate a room that was for rent across town on Derby Street when a rather rumpled black man came over to us, smiled and kindly asked if we were new in town. We said we had come to town to play music. He smiled again and asked what kind of music we played. When we awkwardly replied 'blues,' he smiled even more. I immediately hid behind Jim, smiling. I gave Jim a couple of quick shoves to encourage him to keep talking to this man.

"Jim said we were looking for work," Selby remembered and then she recalled D.C. introducing himself. He was called 'Checotah.'" He continued, asking did we know about the Odyssey, where we could play for tips, or about the Freight and Salvage, where jam night was on Tuesdays? Also there was the Seventh Seal up by campus. 'You can go to the Odyssey and if they like you, you get to come back on a better night and play two sets and pass the hat each time.'

"It sounded great to us," Selby said. "D.C. was a one-man welcoming committee to Berkeley and sent us to bars where we would work for the next four years. They were places where he could also come see us and – unbeknownst to me – follow my development as he changed his life style and worked to evolve his own music."

D.C. remembered, "People kept telling me, 'She's nice, you and Selby ought to get together.' I said I didn't have time to be bothered with Selby. Selby is a liberated female, and I didn't have time for that! I was studyin' music." But still D.C. kept an eye on Selby and Jim. He watched their progress in Berkeley, without Selby knowing, he showed up where she was playing, almost in disguise, since D.C. often experimented with different looks for his performances.

When D.C. recalled this early relationship, he said, "I never had any intentions toward Selby while they were together because I thought so much of Jim." Yet, D.C. told Selby years later that, one lonely night in his cabin on Telegraph, he had written a list of four names on the wall. They were all singers or musicians. He had called it something like his most-qualified-women-in-town-for-me list. At the top of the list was Selby!

One thing Selby remembered was D.C.'s warm smile whenever their paths would cross. She recalled that he finally got her attention by talking to her seriously about his idea of an ideal male / female relationship one night at the Odyssey. "I was passing the hat after my set when he began talking to me." Not being able to hear what he was saying, I said, 'It's too loud, let me finish passing the hat, and then let's go to the balcony

84

upstairs.' He followed me up the narrow stairs so closely I knew what he was thinking!

"We got to the table overlooking the stage below, and he talked of many things. Then he said, 'Neither a man nor a woman can be complete without the other. They are opposite parts of a whole, the woman the more intuitive and the man the more logical; and if they can really trust each other and stand back to back, together they can see the full 360 degrees. There is nothing they cannot do.'" Selby, who had had some unhappy experiences with men in her past, was impressed with D.C.'s take on the relationship between a man and a woman.

Eventually, mutual friends, including Jim, kept trying to push D.C. and Selby toward each other. "Finally they did get us together," D.C. said. "They 'lied' us together. They would exaggerate and tell her I was jumping up and down wanting to meet her and then come and tell me the same thing, trying to fix us up. I had five or six homeless people staying in my broke down cars there in the parking lot at my garage. I'd feed them in the morning and run them out and make them try to do something for themselves, these street people. They were the ones who 'lied' us together. They knew it would be the end of their thing, but they were willing to make that sacrifice for us to get together," D.C. said.

"At the time it finally happened, we had been playing at the same club, but at different times. She was like pure driven snow in a bar full of messups. I knew I had found the right one.

One night, "I told her I was living in a tree. I told her I was missing my tree because I was out of it. She said, 'Tree?' I said, 'Yeah, I have a room up in a tree with thirteen sides on it and thirty feet off the ground.' She just kind of looked at me, like 'This is a good one!' Yet when I asked if she would like to see it sometime, she said she would. We set up a date to get together a couple of weeks later, on her birthday."

D.C. related that, "Before the day came, a friend reminded Selby I was waiting for her at my garage. "It took courage for me to go to the shop that day," Selby said. "This was California, after all. I knew I was stepping off into another world, even though it was within a couple of blocks of where I was living at the time. The shop was very busy, with a good-sized parking lot in front of it, full of cars D.C. was repairing. I stepped inside and the shop was dark and quiet compared to the lot and street outside. As my eyes adjusted, I saw a few guys (standing around). D.C. was a powerful figure just in front of me, squatting down and chopping some wood. A hush fell over the room as his buddies realized who I was."

When D.C. recalled this important date, he remembers what he saw: "Selby was 5'2", slender, her straight, light-brown hair parted in the middle and streaked with natural blonde highlights. She wore no makeup and looked about sixteen years old. She was wearing tight jeans and a black turtleneck sweater. When Selby walked in, I was using a hatchet to chop firewood for the stove. When I saw her, I almost chopped off my thumb! You could see down to the bone. That could have been the end of my career as a musician."

When they met that day in November 1976 at D.C.'s garage, Selby was celebrating her twenty-seventh birthday; D.C. was forty-one. It was the first time they got together anywhere other than a casual meeting in the bar where both of them were working. Selby stayed twenty minutes before going on to dinner with other friends, but they made a date for the next night. He then took her to San Francisco to see a band with a woman she knew playing guitar.

"A few weeks later, I took her to see the tree house I had told her about," D.C. said, "and that gave me credibility." Unfortunately, or maybe fortunately, his van ran out of gas on the way. When he told Selby he would walk to get gas while she waited with his other friends in the van, she said no to that. She would walk with him to get the gas. "That's when I knew she was a keeper," D.C. said. "I considered myself married to Selby from the first time I was with her, but it took her a while to decide to marry me." D.C. had to "cut loose" his five girlfriends and was monogamous the rest of his life.

"That was over thirty years ago," D.C. said in 2007. "It's been beautiful. I was looking for somebody who would do the kind of music I wanted to do. It seemed like a match made in heaven to me." This feeling is reflected in the lyrics written by D.C.

> Oh, baby, I hear voices
> whenever you are near.
> Sweetheart, my heart rejoices
> when you hold me
> hold me tight, Dear.
> Life wasn't real
> Until your heart I can feel.
> The bliss of a sweet romantic kiss,
> The joy you'll never miss.
> Love is a dream, a beautiful dream for two,
> When you find the right one
> to make your dream of love come true!
> (from "Lover's Dream" by D.C. Minner)

"We had to really hunt to find each other," Selby said. "I went from the East Coast to the West Coast, and he went from Oklahoma to the West Coast."

"We didn't waste any time after that," D.C. said. "As soon as we got together and realized who each other was, we took off like a rocket. I knew I wanted a life with her. Soon after we met, she served me soup made from fermented soy beans and seaweed. I looked at what she put in front of me and thought it was a finger bowl. I was thinking, 'Well, she can't cook, but that's okay because I can cook.' But I wasn't marrying her for her cooking anyhow. We had been dating only about four days at that time."

"He was very polite about it," Selby recalled. "He ate the soup, but the man really hates soup to this day. He took me out to eat. I had been waiting for years for a man to take me out to eat," Selby said. "We started at the House of Pancakes on University. D.C. would not let them take the menu away after we ordered. If I so much as looked at something on that menu — a dessert, whatever — he called the waitress over and ordered it.

87

We filled the table with dishes. The hippies who hung out in restaurants hoping to clean up unfinished meals were really eyeballing our table.

"I love to eat and have never even been close to being really thin. So most boys would look at me like, 'If you eat one more bite, I know you'll get fat later on.' I was sick of that guilt trip. D.C. never came close to falling in that trap. He definitely had my attention," she said.

Having already decided he would spend the rest of his life with Selby, D.C. suggested to her that he would like to spend as much time as possible with her. "I could move in your house," D.C. said. "I know it's little, but you won't even know I'm there! I'll put my coat on the last hook and hide my shoes under the bed . . ." Being as D.C. was six feet, 225 pounds, and pretty much a nonstop talker, Selby said, "I really did find those remarks pretty amusing."

After Selby agreed to his moving in, things did turn out a little differently than D.C.'s words had suggested. "Here they came with a piano in the back of a friend's pickup truck!" Selby said. "He came in the yard playing it, with all his friends hanging off it—talk about a motley crew!" D.C. would often sing to Selby, "I hope you've got me where you want me because I'm just where I want to be."

Selby Guenther was entering a place in her life much different from the Rhode Island neighborhood where she lived in an upwardly mobile, middle-class family, and where she had completed three years of art study at the Rhode Island School of Design. She would have a lot to learn and adjust to. But, D.C., who had been keeping an eye on Selby from 1972 until they had gotten together, had already been making many of the changes necessary for him to have a life with her.

D.C. Did a Lot of His Work in Advance

One of the many characteristics that set D.C. apart, particularly after his studies of Eastern philosophy, was his ability to focus on goals, no matter what was happening around him. When he was partying, he partied hard. When he decided to pull himself together, he went to the top of his field. Consciously or unconsciously, D.C. was preparing himself for Selby before she finally came to him.

"I found out long after we were together that he would talk to Jim, find out where we would be playing and come to see what Jim and I were doing with the music," Selby remembered. "I often didn't recognize him. When I first saw D.C., he had dreads way before most people knew what that was. I was fascinated but a little intimidated when he first talked to us. A lot of people were. He was six feet tall, weighed about 230 pounds, and was strong as an ox from lifting car engines and his other work. He once told me he sometimes people would lock their car doors as he walked down the sidewalk on Telegraph Avenue. He was still drinking and he had a lot of anger.

"Anyway, he altered his appearance at will, sometimes being in his stage costume and sometimes in his greasy work clothes," she said. "He called himself Checotah (from the town near where he was born) and started dressing in vaguely Indian-looking clothing. He had a great denim shirt that one of his girlfriends had done fancy embroidery on, doeskin boots with fringe, clothing decorated with Indian nickels. Jim would mention he had seen Checotah when he got back from playing up on campus, and I only vaguely knew who he was talking about.

"Looking back, I think I was somewhat aware of a handsome black man who smiled at me with a beautiful smile whenever he was around," Selby said. "I just wasn't paying much attention to him. He was a lot older than I was, and I never thought of him in terms of romance. In later years, he told me it hurt his feelings when I would walk by him. He said that, although I was polite, I just kept moving, that I 'didn't have time for him.' He was very shy.

"But, as was always his way, he was studying the situation and deciding what he might want to do. After being where I was performing and hearing me sing and talk, he figured out that what I wanted was my music and one good man," Selby said.

"He was old enough and smart enough to know that, if it was ever going to work out with me, he would have to make changes. He'd have to 'do the one-on-one,' as he called it.

"Before we got together, he had cut his hair. He had stopped using hard drugs and hard liquor, though he still drank beer for a couple of years after that. He had already started unraveling from his relationships with other women and was living alone in his shop.

"D.C. had a lot of anger at times in his life," said Selby. "He began turning his anger into a game. He learned to vent his anger in a more intellectual and fun way. In Berkeley, everybody analyzes everything in terms of politics all the time. D.C. would go into a place and get into a group discussion. He would automatically take the other side from the prevailing one. It was like a verbal boxing match for him, mental gymnastics. It was a way that he studied people and incorporated what he learned from his studies of Eastern philosophy into his real life. He didn't ritualistically do the meditation, yoga, or other ceremonial things that Tony (Mathews) did and does. But he took that same knowledge and made it work for him with what mattered to him, which was music and people. He was getting his trip together," she said.

Was D.C. also figuring out what the pretty little blonde singer from the East Coast wanted and deciding whether or not he wanted to give it to her? "You see, I had it all figured out what I would do when I met 'Miss Right' and what I wasn't gonna do," D.C. said in later years. "All that stuff I had been doing earlier was to pacify myself (until she came along)."

Although their friends in Berkeley were happy to see D.C. and Selby together, not everybody was pleased about the relationship of the forty-one-year-old black man and the twenty-seven-year-old blonde woman. Some people referred to Selby as D.C.'s "Little Lolita." "People thought we looked like Little Red Riding Hood and the Big Bad Wolf," D.C. remembered. "They didn't understand why we were together. People said, 'Take her back! Save yourself the trouble. She's too young!' We didn't go

90

around hugging or anything. We just went about our business and let them wonder what our relationship was.

"One time we overheard a remark, and I said, 'We came here to play music and have a good time, but I will box, if you insist.' Most people are looking for respect. You can generally do what you need or want to do if you do it respectfully."

Selby found a refuge in D.C.—a mentor and a charming and skilled guide into the world of blues music. He would transplant her from the vagaries of life as a single female singer in the Bay Area, give her a home, and help her find her life's work. She would be leaving life as she knew it behind to become part of D.C. Minner's world.

D.C., Selby and Their Families

While D.C. was in California, his Aunt Ethel had assumed the responsibility of keeping the home place going. She paid the taxes, and lived on the site for ten years after her mother and sister had died. She always hoped and prayed that D.C. would return to Oklahoma to keep the family's legacy intact and to keep the property, acquired about 80 years earlier, in the family. Ethel knew D.C. was more likely to live on the place if he had a good woman who supported his efforts; she saw that Selby was good for D.C., and so she eagerly welcomed Selby to the family

"The welcome I received in Rentiesville was almost embarrassing in contrast with my family's response to D.C.," Selby said. "My family was always polite to D.C., but D.C.'s Aunt Ethel welcomed me with open arms. She moved us into the family home, which she had had been renting out. She inserted me into the Rentiesville community, cooked us a lot of meals, hired us to fix things so we could have work, and so much more. She courted me, and we had a lot of fun.

"Blacks are far more familiar with white culture than I was with black culture. D.C.'s people were ready for me. Aunt Ethel scooped me up and put me into Rentiesville's African Methodist Episcopal church choir right next to her. That was a fabulous experience for me. None of the singers were professional at all, but they certainly could rock a song. I was 'that little white girl from Rentiesville who sure can sing' when we got to other churches for the Sunday afternoon musicals. They gave me lots of solos and I sang my heart out. It was very affirming. One line into my solo and they would call out 'sing the song', or 'amen,' which was so supportive. I learned a lot."

Early in Selby's relationship with D.C., they also visited Altonia Ferguson Nutter. She was D.C.'s first wife Doris' great aunt, the family called her Sister, and she had been raising D.C.'s children since Doris had died. Sister was a formidable older woman and would get right to the point in a conversation. When she met Selby, she said, "What are you doing here?" Selby was startled by her bluntness, but said, "I am in love with D.C." Sister gave her no problem after that. "Sister was an educator and a seamstress and was still very well put together: gold-rimmed glasses and a well-kept wig," Selby said. "Her house had those dark moldings popular in the fifties and smelled of wonderful food." She had been the driving force for Rentiesville to have a school of its own where she was the principal. In addition to her being a leader in the town's education she was involved in civic duties as the town's treasurer.

In D.C.'s immediate family, his daughter Sheila welcomed Selby to the family and called her "little mom." D.C.'s son Tony left Oklahoma soon after he graduated from college and returned only for his Aunt Altonia's funeral in 1993. After he was an adult, Tony had no relationship with D.C. He was polite to D.C. in public but would have nothing to do with him otherwise. However, Tony renewed his relationship with Selby shortly before D.C.'s death in 2010. "Right before he died," Selby said, "he put his arm around me and said, 'my stepmother.' It was very touching."

D.C. had finally located his father in Stockton, California, and met him for the second time when D.C. was 33. After he and Selby got together, he took Selby to meet his father and stepmother. "He liked me," Selby said. "He told me, 'if you ever

92

need anything, call me.' D.C. was completely surprised and commented that his dad had never said that to him!"

Where joining the Minner family had been quick and fairly easy for Selby, joining the Guenthers was a different story for D. C. "The hardest thing (about the relationship with D.C.) was my family," Selby said. "They didn't want to understand. They were distant, but polite, to D.C. I thought it would take about three years, maybe, for them to accept the relationship. It took ten! This was embarrassing to me since his family was so warm to me.

"I had been designated the family black sheep years earlier because of my behavior on other issues. Being against the Vietnam War was a fight at our house. Going to art school was a battle. My being a musician was a shock. So this was just one more thing. I was the first born child, and they were learning to be parents on me. I moved three thousand miles away from home as soon as possible after I got out of college to learn the blues and to have space to be myself."

Selby's sister Jean, a psychosynthesis counselor and founder of the Vermont Center for Psychosynthesis, showed up in California soon after D.C. and Selby got together. "She seemed very involved with him (D.C.)," Jean recalled. "I remember thinking that it wasn't going to be easy for me to get to know him."

"When the visit was drawing to a close," Selby said. 'Jean had an odd request. She wanted to see Jim, of all people!' I had not seen him much in the two-and-a-half years since we broke up," Selby said.

Jim Donovan, the man Selby had come to California with, had a new German girlfriend by this time. But, "she (Jean) insisted," Selby said. "I called Jim and explained the situation. Rita invited Jean, D.C., and me in for tea. So we trailed into the kitchen and sat around a table by the window. Finally, Jean made her move. 'Jim, what do you think of my sister's relationship with D.C.?' I was taken aback. An impertinent request, it seemed to me.

"All eyes were on Jim," Selby remembered, "and he did not miss the moment. He grinned and firmly stated, 'I think it's a match made in heaven.' That was it. I was thrilled. He got it! He was not afraid to state it. It was true, and I was grateful for his candor . . . I could have jumped up and hugged him! Of course, I didn't, but he sure deserved a hug!"

Of Selby's parents, Jean said, "Our folks were upset. Selby, their firstborn 'perfect child,' at least until she finished high school, was living with a guy, and he was a musician. They were afraid she was committing herself to being a poor musician, and they didn't like it that he was also black. How much further from their hopes for her could their daughter go? They wanted Selby to use her art education from Rhode Island School of Design that they had worked hard to pay for and perhaps use her great voice secondarily, but NOT to back up someone else. It wasn't a life style they could relate to, and they were worried about her not earning a living and not taking 'good enough' care of herself. D.C. brought to the family more changes from their expectations for Selby than they initially felt they could deal with. In addition, they also were afraid Selby might negatively influence their youngest child, Hilary, who was still in grade school."

Jean remembered their dad saying, "How could she change so much? She used to be such a good girl!" After she got over the first shock, Selby's mother, Dortha, did try to persuade her husband to give the relationship a chance. "Well, you know she did everything our way for twenty years. Now I think she is going to do things her way for a while. Maybe we should give her a chance to make this work."

"In the long haul, I think they came to terms with her choices of mate and music," Jean said. "They found things they could relate to and admire. They, also, had 'followed their dreams' and could see the hard work and sacrifices D.C. and Selby were making, as they had, to live the life they wanted to live. They came to see how much D.C. and Selby loved each other and how well they lived and worked together, 24/7, exactly as my parents had lived as a married couple. Over time, the power of love and commonality took precedence."

Selby said, "When my folks decided to accept D.C., my mother told me, 'Well, you and D.C. have done everything you said you were going to do and have gone where you said you were going to go and have accomplished all your goals.'

"I give my family a lot of credit," Selby said. "They have grown and come around a hundred percent, but it took longer than I expected. I thought it might take about three years for them to accept D.C. It took about ten, but they all grew to love D.C. They realized he was good for me and good to me and that was enough, finally."

On the Road Again, Making Music: Doing It Their Way

Within weeks of their first date, D.C. and Selby had decided to hit the road making music together. Selby had said she wanted to leave Berkeley. D.C. told her he would take her anywhere she wanted to go.

Selby remembered the promise D.C. made outside the Odyssey where they would be playing later that night. "Our sax player Lauree had just 'married us' in front of the small stage in there. 'Do you take this man to be your lawful wedded husband? Say I do!! Say I do!!' he insisted. 'Yes,' cautiously I replied. Then to D.C., 'Do you take this woman to be your wife?' 'I do,' he answered calmly. I said, 'Well, let's walk around the block for a honeymoon.' D.C. answered me, 'Fine.'

"We went to the corner of University and San Pablo a few doors north and turned up University where the traffic rushed by in the early evening, and I said, 'This is fine, but I am planning to leave town sometime soon. I just have to get out of Berkeley. 'Where do you want to go?' D.C asked. 'I don't know,' I paused, 'maybe back to Rhode Island.' D.C. said, 'I'll take you there!' That sounded too good to be true. I grinned; we grabbed hands, finished our walk back to the bar with one of the best PA systems in town and did our set."

His mechanic's business had become so successful that a bit of sacrifice was involved when D.C. left it behind. Selby used some money she had to buy a drum set and a sound system. D.C. played guitar and sang. Selby played bass and sang. They hired drummers in towns along the way.

"We were doing a trip that hadn't been done before, because we were going to towns and then getting a job," D.C. said. "The rest of the blues bands were using agents and had the jobs before they got to town. Within six months, we were playing six times a week. We stayed on the road for twelve years, in that manner.

Those twelve years hold many stories. "Our first stop was Bisbee, Arizona," D.C. remembered. "We got the first gig of our own together there, and we're still playing that same gig almost 30 years later (in 2007). We played at St. Elmo's and The Brewery; Selby and me and a guy named Scott went in there. Later, we left town and Scott stayed there. Trying to get Selby squared away on bass, (she had been playing guitar when they got together), we stopped at tiny little towns. We went into the woods and played, too. Selby and me and Lauree Watkins got together and called ourselves the International Boogie Woogie Blues Band."

One night, the International Boogie Woogie Blues Band driving between jobs were pulled over by a state trooper. D.C. was driving the van, but he had been drinking beer earlier, so he had Selby, who was in the front seat with him, switch to the driver's seat. The trooper asked her for the driver's license. Selby handed him hers. The trooper said, "No, I want the driver's license. Even in the dark, I can tell the difference between a large black man and a little white woman!" He then ordered everybody out of the van.

The saxophone player, who had also been drinking, was a little bitty man with a goatee and a beard which stuck straight out. He walked up to this state trooper, looked way up at him, pointing upward with that beard, and said indignantly "You cannot stop us! You cannot stop us! We are the International Boogie Woogie Blues Band. Do you understand the meaning of the word international!?!" The trooper was so amused that he turned to Selby and said, "Just get 'em out of here. And I want you to drive."

That was easier said than done. Selby didn't know how to drive a five-speed stick shift, so D.C. coached her to use a clutch. She kept trying, but over and over again but she killed the engine, as the trooper stood by watching her. Finally, with D.C. telling her, "Give it some gas now!" she gunned the engine and took off backwards, right toward the trooper's car, stopping just inches from hitting it. Finally, with D.C. holding his breath, Selby shifted into drive and slowly and carefully got back on the highway, leaving the trooper still standing by his car, shaking his head and laughing.

Another time they had been invited to play at a community center in a rural area by doctors and other volunteers who had come up from Albuquerque on a regular basis to build a healing center at Picuris Pueblo, just south of Taos. There were a lot of substance abuse problems, as well as other challenges. The doctors involved were determined to create a new center that would incorporate both western and native medicines.

"We arrived in the afternoon with the old step van D.C. had bought in Berkeley and sprayed robin-egg blue," Selby said. "We could only go about 45 mph at best, so we started early in the day up through the mountains north of Santa Fe.

"Mid-afternoon we rolled into the pueblo. No one was in sight, though there were adobe buildings all around. We found our way to the health center. We were told this was the right place, the doctors there told us. 'You don't see the people, but they see you. They are in their houses—some of them are getting over last night.'

"So we backed up to the community center in the middle of everything, hauled in the sound system and amps and guitars and the drum set, set it all up and did the sound check," Selby recalled. "We played a couple of songs, pretty loud, and got back in the truck to relax and pick out our clothes for the show. We had a young female guitarist with us who could play some nice lead parts.

"Finally the day ended and evening fell. We went back inside and started our show. People came trickling in, young and old and babies and children. We weren't the greatest musicians at that point, but we tried hard. Our enthusiasm was contagious. Gradually people separated themselves from the crowd and started to dance to this 'different' kind of music.

"The veins stood out on D.C.'s neck as he sang, 'We're gonna rock this place tonight, rock it till the broad day light'," Selby said. "I cranked up the bass. As the night wore on it became clear that this group was not going to wiggle and sachet in a series of individualistic dance statements like we were used to seeing. They came on the dance floor as a group and they moved as a group, babies and elders and all in between—not partnered but revolving in a circle around and around the floor. They were so together that they rocked the house as much as we did with the electric guitars and trap (drum) set. It changed the music— the way they danced together pulled our rhythm and purified it somehow with its deliberate simplicity. It was a great night.

"At the end, we were tearing down and visiting with those who came up to the stage. A young thirty-ish woman particularly liked D.C. She spoke to him shyly a while and then invited him to come with her for some Koolaid. That blew his mind."

D.C. said later, "I've had a lot of invitations before, but never for Koolaid!"

"We chalked it up to someone trying to live alcohol-free but still be hospitable and sociable," Selby remembered, "We packed up and drove back to town."

"Eventually we worked our way back here (to Oklahoma) and picked up an old drummer friend of mine, Vernon Powers," D.C. said. "We started calling ourselves Blues On the Move, as we knew we'd always be on the move. It's necessary to be on the move when you don't have your musical identity yet. In a local bar, they'll start calling out your songs, and they get you in a rut. It takes much longer to develop your personal style, without travel, much longer. When you travel, you can do the same material and get it strong, because it's freshly rehearsed. You do it over and over and the tighter it gets. The road is good for that. We played from California, Oregon, and Washington all the way across to Massachusetts, New York, and Rhode Island. We stayed on the road pretty much nonstop until 1988. We created our own touring circuit."

"We pride ourselves on our independence," Selby said. "We guarded that jealously. Never borrow money, no fulltime jobs, no career jobs except the music. Financial independence gives you your time back. An artist's most valuable possession is free time. No expensive living situations.

"I always loved waking up in a different place," she said. "You always have the hope that the next gig will be the best—the one that gives you a big audience or a recording deal or better musicians to work with. Moving is a big part of that. The magic is just over the hill, so being on the road is exhilarating. Anything can happen next! When performing is paying all your bills and taking you through countless new situations, it's your calling card. You run into some great folks who really love what you do. You make good friends along the way, people you just met who will take you home and put you up and leave in the morning for work and just ask you to lock the door when you leave."

It also helps to be fearless. "People had often said to us, 'They would love you in Europe! You should go there,' Selby recalled. "We also wanted to see our friend Simm in Belgium, who had been calling asking us to come visit. So in 1994, I made countless overseas calls. CDs were new; we had no CD out, only a cassette release. In the early nineties and no agent would book us without a CD, but I was told by one woman in Belgium who owned Der Kleine Nachtmusic, 'Get here, come see us, and I'll give you a job.'

"We just bought a ticket and packed fourteen suitcases and took off," D.C. said. "People say, 'You ain't got no jobs!' I say, 'We'll get jobs when we get there. First you got to get there.' Soon after arriving in Belgium, we went to the Banana Peel

Blues Club and met Eric Kuralt, the owner. He could not give us a job because he was booked three months ahead, and we were not going to be there long enough. But the next morning, he sent me a fax that listed 50 clubs which hired blues acts and included their phone numbers. The clubs were in Northern France, Belgium, and Holland. I called them all, and we wound up getting eight gigs in Belgium and Holland." Selby and D.C. rented a car and an apartment and spent two months traveling, sightseeing, and visiting friends in Europe. They paid for their trip by performing.

Most of D.C and Selby's friends were amazed by their nomadic lifestyle. Selby's sophisticated, reserved New Englander mother sent them a little box of juggling balls. On the outside of the box was the title: "More Balls Than Most!" Years later, she could hardly believe she had sent them that. Eventually, the time came for them to settle down when D.C. would finally assume the role in the family that Miss Lura had expected him to fill in Oklahoma.

Below: D.C. And Selby Minner in Arcata CA.
Photo by Elaine Grosso

Blues on the Move: D.C., Selby, Vernon Powers.
First photo shoot, Albuquerque Train Station.
Photo byInez Foose circa 1981.

Top: The Band Bus named Buck 1977, 78. Sign painted by Selby
Inez Foose photo at the Golden Inn, Golden NM

Below: Building it in in Berkeley on Tenth St photo: Sue Young

Cerrillos NM.
D.C.
Selby Minner
Vernon Powers

Blues On The Move
mostly lived in California
(also AZ, NM) from
1976 until 1988, and then
continued to tour the
South West and West
Coast every year or two
until 2006.

Cerrillos NM.
A very early
band shot
D.C.
Selby Minner
Vernon Powers
Rick Pruitt.

Top: Selby at a gig, Pioneer Square, Seattle circa 1978.

Below: with her Grandmother Grace Selby in Des Moines IA, summer of 1976.

Selby in Bisbee, AZ at St. Elmo's in Brewery Gulch.
Photo by Richard Byrd

(L) At the Mexican border in AZ south of Bisbee by Richard Byrd —the most published photo of Blues on the Move.

(R) Bronze statue by Selby created from photo. Made at Bacone College in Muskogee, OK.

Drawings by D.C.
D.C. taught Selby to play bass;
she returned the favor by teaching him to draw!

Mrs. Dortha Selby Guenther Mershon of Portsmouth, RI.
Selby's Mom.

Dan "Oklahoma Slim" Ortiz lives at the Hall of Fame now. He is a guitarist of note and Selby's boyfriend, helping her keep these dreams alive and moving forward more than ten years after Mr. Minner's death.

Below: Stained glass window designed by Selby Minner, created by artist Ron Wood of Checotah OK.

Selby gets to
induct Miss
Blues into
the OJHOF!

Shiron Ray (Barebones Film Festivals), Jeanetta Calhoun Mish (OK State Poet Laureate, & Mongrel Empire Press), and Selby Minner at 2017 Oklahoma Arts Council Conference in Enid.

Sue Selby Guenther leaves from the new house for her
first day of Kindergarten in Rumford, R..I.

Chapter 5: Back Home to Rentiesville

Fell into a Trap

By 1988 D.C. and Selby's Blues On The Move band had been on the road for twelve years, having built up a circuit from the Pacific Northwest to the East Coast and back again, always passing through Oklahoma, coming and going.

"We'd come to Oklahoma and fix cars, paint signs and do other odd jobs, and save our money," Selby said. "Then we would hit the road to go to the next place we could work." For years, their only Oklahoma venue besides Rentiesville was in the OU campus town of Norman, at the Library Bar. They played there coming and going through Oklahoma every tour.

"Once in the late 70's we got a gig in Tulsa, at a bar," she added. "But it was a rock bar and people didn't even clap for us. That was a short set," Selby remembered. "We didn't fit in at the rock club.

"After that, we went to a jam session on the white side of town, D.C., Vernon and I. The guy introduced us by saying 'I want you to give these guys a big hand. I don't know if I would have the nerve to go and play on the north (black) side of town!' Since D.C. and Vernon both believed that you know a person by their fears, this made the hair stand up on their heads. It made us very nervous that they were afraid of black people. We played two songs and beat a hasty retreat. There was very little work for us in Oklahoma, except in the college towns, Norman and Stillwater, where people were more openminded. That was about '78 or '79," she said, "before the blues societies were formed in

Tulsa and in Oklahoma City." Those associations changed the atmosphere for blues music in Oklahoma.

"So, for a long time, we would occasionally come to Oklahoma for a month or two, then rent out the house and leave again for a year or so," Selby said. "We would always make it a point to try to get back for Memorial Day weekend when the Rentiesville Cemetery Committee held a reunion and would hire us to perform. That would pay for our trip back here."

In 1988, the Minners returned to Oklahoma intending to stay over for six weeks, prior to performances planned in Norway, and "We fell into the trap my grandmother set for us—free rent!" D.C. said. "We had free rent. You offer a musician free rent, and he'll live damn near anywhere! After she died, it was time to come back here, because I'm the head of the family now. There was a vacuum here (with my older relatives dying off). I've got grandkids and great-grandkids running around here. They need that legacy about family tradition to carry on, and that's what my job was. I could have been sitting somewhere on a mountain top in a state of bliss. But that would have been a selfish move, considering that I had brought two kids into the world and enticed them to love me. So I got back here in time, before my oldest auntie died, to take over.

"But I'll say this," he added. "Anything you do that is that important, you have multiple reasons to do it. One of the reasons was, it was my watch to come back here and look out for the gene pool of my family. We owned property here. We had a house here. It's centrally located. We have real weather here. I can be myself here; I don't have to put on. Everybody knows who I am.

"Also, when we had started touring, the only music being played in the Tulsa area was country and rock. Between 1977 and 1988, two blues societies were formed in Oklahoma and fourteen blues clubs opened. So when you put all those pieces together, they said move back to Oklahoma."

"We had been in L.A. for a year and a half, working five nights a week," D.C. said. "We got a gig in Norway and had about six weeks before we had to be in New York to go, so we came back to Oklahoma to see about the place and the family. We were here a couple of weeks and got to talking about the differences between L.A. and here. We looked at each other and said this is pretty nice." "Yeah, green," Selby remembered saying. "No helicopters," D.C. said. "After a few days, I said to Selby, 'Do you really want to go to Norway?'"

"People are friendly here, the air is clean, and it's in the center of the country," Selby said of their decision to stay. "You can head out in all directions quickly, and I loved to travel. Then I got to know the community, and they were so warm to me. They had me singing in the choir, the whole thing.

"I like it that two people could make a difference in a place like this," Selby added. "In California, it would take either a lot of people or a lot of money to get something done. Here two people, with energy and determination, can make a difference. All you have to do is commit and get busy."

D.C. and Selby knew it would take a lot of work to make their dream of making a life and a living playing blues in Oklahoma come true, but they were used to that. "We work hard, but we work together," D.C. said. "We found as long as we're together, there's really no problem we can't handle."

It was fun, but it wasn't easy.

Upon their arrival home in Rentiesville in 1988, they got a shock. D.C.'s family home had been rented to a local minister's sister, Pearlene. The woman had five boys and a fourteen year-old daughter.

"She spent the days praying so loudly people could hear it out on the road, and she left the supervision of the boys to her daughter," Selby said. "The place was in ruins. It smelled. It had every kind of roach imaginable–the plumbing was stopped up. The bathroom sink was hanging off the wall. The septic tank in the backyard was an open sewer. The trash pile out back was twenty-five feet long. Every light switch and door knob in the house was broken."

D.C. told the woman and her brother, the preacher, that they would have to leave. The preacher told the members of his church that "the devil had attacked him!" But, the people in Rentiesville were relieved to see the preacher go. They told stories of being pelted with rocks by the five unruly boys when they drove by the house. Neighbors had begun to call the preacher's church a cult.

Selby cried at the disrepair of the house, but D.C. said, "As long as they left the studs, we are okay. I can fix it." The first thing he did was pick up the trash in the yard and replace broken sheet rock. He bought fourteen bug bombs and set them off in the house, the attic, and under the floors. Then D.C. and Selby hit roaches with fly swatters for weeks as they repainted the entire interior of the house.

About the time the Minners finished restoring the house, they learned there was soon to be a big Civil War reenactment – the first one at Honey Springs, less than a quarter mile away from their location. Honey Springs was the site of the largest military clash ever to have occurred in Oklahoma. The clash between Union and Confederate troops took place July 17, 1863, and was the pivotal point of the Civil War in Indian Territory.

"We decided to try an experiment," Selby said. They had attracted a good crowd to a party at their location on Memorial Day and were encouraged by the response of local people to their music. So, they spruced up D.C.'s grandmothers old store with yellow paint and created a party room. D.C. cooked four briskets. A neighbor shared her famous potato salad recipe (she used onion soup mix instead of onions, so it kept better). They opened up during the reenactment, offering live music and selling barbeque dinners.

"People came by and ate," Selby said. "They loved the music, and D.C. saw an opportunity." Grandma Lura's Cozy Corner had closed twenty years earlier when she passed away. Maybe reopening the bar as a music venue with a stage in it would be a solution to staying in Oklahoma and making music for a living at the same time. 'Opening our own retail outlet' as D.C would refer to it. Selby took some persuading.

Although D.C. had stopped drinking years before, Selby had memories of bad times when alcohol had been a problem for D.C. She was reluctant to own a bar and have alcohol in the house all the time, fearing it might present too much temptation for a reformed drinker to handle. But, after a couple of weeks, D.C. managed to convince Selby he was up to the challenge, and she relented. Labor Day weekend was their target date for opening.

"So we started tearing down every wall we had just recently repainted," Selby said. "What a mess! Years of dust and pulverized sheet rock piled everywhere, the big pretty kitchen gone to get more space for the club. The bath tub came out, and a ladies' room emerged with two stalls. A stage and a bar were built. We had thirty days until Labor Day weekend, and the race was on!"

With that first opening, the Down Home Blues Club was born, and the stage was set for their later creation of the Dusk Til Dawn Blues Festival, held at Rentiesville every Labor Day since 1991.

"You're the Dumbest Dummy in the World!"

"When we had gotten here to stay the first time, in 1979, we opened up a grocery store, a little convenience store," D.C. said. "Selby's daddy gave her a $1,000, and, instead of a wedding, we took that and opened up a little place. This is a mixed community, and I didn't know how they would treat my bride, my mixed-couple bride. They would ring the doorbell. I'd go hide. She'd come out to wait on them, and I'd eavesdrop to hear, because they could be insulting her and she wouldn't know it, because she's from back east. But I know by the tone of their voice what they mean. I've never been so proud of a group of people in my life as I was of my community and the way they accepted her.

"Then we opened the club (The Down Home Blues Club) in 1988," D.C. said in an interview for Living Blues magazine in 1998. "We were always too small; it was just the house. I'm known for thinking ahead, and I said, 'I have to enlarge this club before my business smothers itself, because it's coming too fast and I have to turn people away. I had one old house and I begged up on another one and somebody gave me another one. I tore them down and pulled the nails out of them, drug them down and put them back together, built this place and more than doubled the size of the club. Part of the place is my great-great-grandfather's house that I tore down. There's a lot of tradition down on that corner," D.C. told interviewers Dr. George Carney and Dr. Hugh Foley in the magazine interview.

"When I was up on the roof putting shingles on it in 100 degree heat, some of my friends drove by, laughing and saying things like 'Come fishing with us, D., you're the dumbest dummy in the world! Ain't nobody coming out here!' Even Selby was reluctant at first. But I grew up with people bringing their money in here and laying it on the counter, so this seemed normal to me. I was confident it would work. From the day we opened up, we had a good business.

"Then, the first night I opened, here comes one of those so-called friends wanting me to let him in on credit. I said, 'Not you. Of all people, not you. You almost made me quit. You made me feel so bad that day, I tell you, coming around here drinking and having so much fun while I worked. I almost put my hammer down.'"

Terrell Lester, an entertainment writer for the *Tulsa World* newspaper, wrote the following description of the Minners' Rentiesville establishment:

> Hot links, hot licks and hot times. The Down Home Blues Club at Rentiesville has it all. Heaping helpings of everything to keep a person licking fingers and tapping toes from nightfall to sunrise. D.C. Minner and his wife, Selby, are cooking when they are in the kitchen

or on the stage. They smoke the beef and turn up the heat on the blues. It's a way of life for the Minners and the time of their lives for their customers.

The Down Home Blues Club is a simple and unpretentious roadhouse. It hugs the only road through Rentiesville... On weekend nights, the population of Rentiesville might double, as people from Tulsa and Tahlequah and McAlester and Muldrow follow the sounds and aromas to the little white frame building at the end of an asphalt road. Between songs and between sets, Selby might sell a beer, serve some hot links or collect a cover charge. There are women in high heels and women in sneakers. There are men in cowboy boots and in patent-leather loafers. There are sunglasses at midnight and beer bottles at sunup. They dance the two-step and the bop. They do the stroll and they do the twist. Some men lead and some women lead. Some have rhythm. Some don't know how to spell it. The ceilings are low and Christmas lights stay strung year 'round. The room is as clean as it is bright.

Selby said Lester's article in the Tulsa newspaper resulted in the Minners having all the business they could handle at their club.

D.C. and Selby also became very much involved in the community. "I used to do a local radio show three days a week," D.C. said. "We played gospel music on Sundays. I'd do a show for seniors: who is dead, where the funeral is, who is preaching, who is singing. A guy we knew came home from Kansas City to see his mother and was at her house on Sunday morning when our show came on at 8 a.m. He said she woke him up and said, 'Come on, you got to get up. D.C. is on the radio.' He said, 'Mama, I can hear it from here.' She said, 'No! You got to come in here!' She wanted him to watch the radio!" This radio show

121

spread the word to the local community and filled the club with customers.

But D.C.'s dreams went beyond simply opening and operating a blues club. "We used to be riding down the road on tour somewhere out west and I'd say, 'Someday I'm going to start a festival,'" D.C. recalled, in an interview with Drs. George Carney and Hugh Foley in 1998. "Selby and the drummer used to say, 'yeah, yeah,' but they didn't really believe it like I did. I've always had this dream in the back of my head of doing the festival . . . We've met a lot of people across the country who played good music and never have had a break and have never been heard and they're just as good as anybody we've ever seen... Well, I've got all those guys I know can play real well. If I can get them together in one place, that'll be a festival.

"So I call them and talk to all of them and told them I didn't have any money to give 'em, would they all come and play on the same day? They said, 'yeah,' and I said, 'Well, next time, I'll pay you.' So they all came down and volunteered their time. And we did our first blues festival, and it was a huge success. We had 750 people and seven bands, which was a big, big, big deal. So then it just grew out of there. Our budget is so small (when we started), we don't have the luxury of planning anything we want. We have to see who's available or who hasn't been here or who's in the area, are they in our price range or who's willing to come at that reduced price.

"But that's changing. (In 1996) we had Eddie Kirkland. He got on his manager when he got back to New Jersey and said, 'I want to play more places like that, man! I want you to stop sending me to those damn stuffed shirt places!' In 1995, we saw close to 4,000 people."

There have been festivals at D.C. and Selby's home and in what used to be a cotton field out back every year since 1991, bringing to Rentiesville as many as 5,000 visitors on Labor Day weekends. The Dusk til Dawn Blues Festival in recent years has employed at least thirty bands each year that are eager to perform at the venue in a town with a population of fewer than one hundred people. Selby figured out that the Dusk til Dawn festivals had paid about half a million dollars to some four thousand musicians by their twentieth year.

"The Rentiesville festival has turned into a reunion of sorts for fans and musicians alike," the Minners' web site notes. "A showcase for great regional blues bands headed up by (a number of) international stars–many on the move up through the ranks and proud to be included in the Rentiesville tradition–and a focus for the music-loving community across the state and beyond. It's also a place for other people to play: people who are deserving but no one will hire them because they haven't sold any records."

"We make it so if it's good for us, it's good for everybody," D.C. said. "All the churches are welcome to bring their stuff down here and sell it. We spread the money. We try to attract as much money as possible to McIntosh County. We try to be community oriented, and they work with us. You see them people out there working their butts off during the festivals." "We fill up the motels," Selby said.

In addition, the Minners have made their festival family-friendly. They offer a "Kids Village," complete with African storytelling with conga drums that all the kids can participate in playing. Making pottery, doing face painting, wearing costumes, and other child-friendly activities are available throughout the festivals.

Tom Yearnshaw of the *Blues Festival Guide* described it this way in his article, "It's Just a Family Affair:"

> The 16th Annual Dusk Til Dawn Blues Festival was held over this past Labor Day weekend in the Rentiesville, Oklahoma back yard and home of founders DC and Selby Minner, Back yard and Home??? That's Right!!! But there's a story here. Tradition, too.

> Years ago, DC's grandmother ran a "corn whiskey house" on this hallowed site in rural

123

Oklahoma. When DC and Selby decided to take some of the "move" out of their roadweary band, "Blues On The Move," DC grabbed Selby and headed "back home," where they moved into Grandma's old place, settled into the 'quiet life in the country' (HA!!!), and set part of their house aside to be 'The Down Home Blues Club'.

Dusk Til Dawn—that's 5 PM to 5 AM, folks, 'cause it's usually warm in Rentiesville in the daytime—grew from its origins as an annual event at the club. A few years back, as the show got bigger, DC and Selby converted their unofficial not-for-profit child into a full-fledged, official 501(c)(3) nonprofit 'teenager,' including many from their dedicated 'family' of volunteers on the Board.

Everything about Dusk Til Dawn is a 'family' affair. The Minners are still very dedicated and integral to the show, taking the lead role in organizing and presenting the event and in performing twice nightly for the three-day show. Their extended 'family' includes 12 Board Members, over 100 volunteers, and thousands of dedicated fans. Many of these folks have been returning each year since the very beginning.

Several weeks before the show, volunteers, some who come several thousand miles to help, begin to work the magic that transforms the 'back forty' into the festival site. Three-foot tall grasses are mowed into a comfortable 'lawn.' Power is run so vendors can sell t-shirts, jewelry, barbeque, fried fish, candy, ice cream, and even 'fried pies.' The Kid's Village sprouts up around an old school bus (the Kid's Village is just too much and gets a paragraph of its own below), and a circus-sized tent miraculously appears before the main outdoor stage to complete the 'mirage.' The "Down Home Blues Club," which is now in semiretirement and only open once a month, gets a quick dusting, some posters and lights to liven its interior, and its Festival time.

This year's show presented 30 bands on three stages over the three-day run. The mix, as it has been from the beginning, was rich in the Oklahoma blues tradition (James Walker, Tony Matthews, and Berry Harris — to name just a few) but also included national and regional acts such as Rory Block, James Peterson, and Johnny Rawls. The line up even included several groups of young blues musicians (age 16) from as far away as Dallas, and to keep things moving between acts, a rich variety of acoustic blues was presented throughout the evening.

In keeping with DC's and Selby's active participation in the Oklahoma school system through their innovative 'Blues in the Schools' programs, the Kid's Village has also been a big part of the event. Face painting, costumes, 'dragons' (a la Chinese New Year's parades), clay pottery, and puppet shows are made lovingly available by a group of exceptional volunteers. These are all hands-on activities, keeping young minds occupied while the hypnotic sounds of blues slowly soak into the young minds that will be the future of the blues. This Kid's Village is unlike anything we've seen before!!!

Around 5 AM Monday morning, the mirage begins to fade. The corner of Rentiesville Road and DC Minner Road slowly begins its

125

transformation back to a peaceful country corner, the echoes of 30 great bands being slowly absorbed into the still Oklahoma dawn. The Down Home Blues Club lets out a slow sigh as it slips back into the comfort of semiretirement, and the grasses are already starting to grow back. But this is truly a play land with a once-a-year mission to spread its owner's vision of The Blues far and wide.

There are fitting footnotes to this story and to DC and Selby Minner's long devotion to the blues tradition. Over the weekend, Selby Minner (along with Elvin Bishop, Junior Markham, Steve Pryor, James Walker, and Frank Swain) was inducted into the Oklahoma Blues Hall of Fame, DC Minner received a "Lifetime Achievement Award" from the Oklahoma Blues Hall of Fame, and September 1, 2006 was declared DC Minner Day throughout Oklahoma by Governor Brad Henry. 'Congratulations' are indeed in order for all.

After saying goodbye to our new found family in Rentiesville we're back on the road in Blues Country and will keep you posted.

The Dusk til Dawn Blues Festival is the longest-running three day blues festival in the history of Oklahoma. But the club and the festival are only a fraction of the contribution D.C. and Selby made to their community, their state, and the nation.

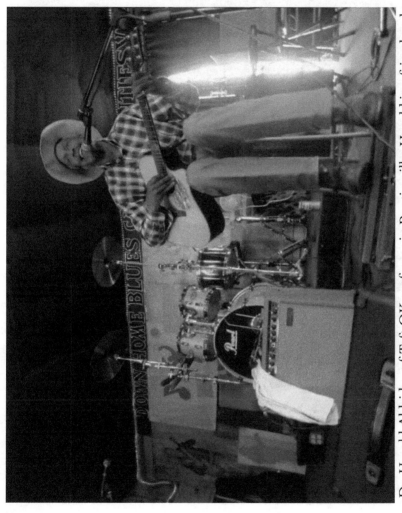

Dr. Harold Aldridge of Taft OK performs in Rentiesville. Harold is a friend and had the presence of mind to recordD.C. telling his stories. Many of his interviews are used in this book.

Chuck and Sandra Sauer Family and friends in Hayfork CA Their band is called the Family Band

D.C. onstage in his Rentiesville
Down Home Blues Club
circa 1989

Close friend
Leroy Goudeau,
working the door
to collect entry fee.

Nappy Brown, Selby and D.C. At the Tulsa Blues Society Festival.
This night they performed and also met Little Johnny Taylor, Nappy
("Night Time is the Right Time") and Johnny Rawls. This Festival
motivated the start of the Rentiesville Blues Fest in 1991

D.C. Minner and Blues on
the Move with Selby at
Juneteenth on Greenwood
in Tulsa
Tulsa World Photo

Juneteenth on
Greenwood with Big
Dave Carr on Sax,
backing up Lowel Fulson
when he was inducted
into the Oklahoma Jazz
Hall Of Fame circa 1989.

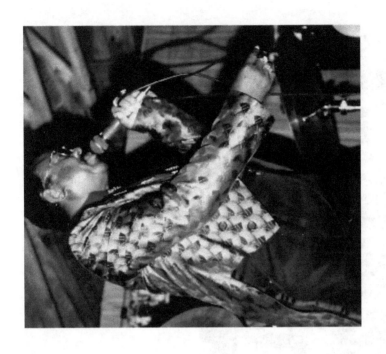

(R)Little Johnny Taylor DD '91

D.C. MINNER AND BLUES ON THE MOVE WITH SELBY

(L) Oklahoma Jazz Hall of Fame Inductee 1999

Flash Terry, Donna "Lady D" Brewer, Frank Swain 1991
At the first Rentiesville Dusk til Dawn Blues Festival They played here many many times.

Larry Johnson in CA. He won the Guitar Showdown at the Rentiesville Fest, documented on CD.

D.C. at the Edmond Blues Festival, Photo: Fred W. Marvel

D.C. Minner, circa early 2000s (Courtesy *Tulsa World*)

James Peterson played the Rentiesville Blues Festival for many years!

Top: Selby's relatives come in from coast to coast to help at the Festival.. Cousin Jim Selby and brother Louis Guenther keep the ticket booth running smoothly as the crowd arrives.
Photo by Jerry Willis

Below: Rentiesville Dusk to Dawn Blues Festival

Top: Down Home Blues Club

Below: The Festival site / Minner homestead in Rentiesville, OK

D.C., DW Moore, and Daniel Williams help the non profit, Friends of Rentiesville Blues Inc., get ready for the yard-sale fundraiser. We all lifted D.C. up onto that amp—the awning will provide shade when he performs with the band.

Walter BBQs at the Fest

Into the future: Akeem Kemp rocks the main stage at the festival.

Smoke House Bob sets up his Bar-b-que stand at the Festival.

VENUE - *Cains Ballroom* - Tulsa, OK

ARTIST - *Kelli O'Hara* - Elk City, OK

ARTIST - *D.C. Minner* - Rentiesville, OK

"Rhythm & Routes Oklahoma Music Trail inductee D.C. Minner dedicated his life to the blues.

After decades of touring the country, he returned to his birthplace of Rentiesville, OK where he and his wife, Selby, launched the now famous Dusk Till Dawn Blues Festival in 1991.

This year's festival is the Friday, Saturday and Sunday of Labor Day Weekend at the end of the summer."

D.C. Performs at his Down Home Blues Club in Rentiesville

146

CHAPTER 6: WORKING WITH KIDS

Blues in the Schools

Their impact on their Rentiesville community and their state of Oklahoma is a palpable contribution, but one that is immeasurable is what D.C. and Selby have done for young people. From the 1970's until 2006 as part of the Blues in Schools program, they traveled across America using music and their life experiences to teach mostly, at-risk kids how to have a better life. They worked both with individual classes and with student assemblies. They were honored in 1999 by the International Blues Foundation representing105 blues societies in 27 countries, for their work in schools.

"They flew us back to Washington, D.C.," D.C. said about receiving the award. "There I was, in the same place with four or five of those politicians I'd sworn I was going to choke if I was ever in the room with them, and I couldn't touch 'em! Photo ops is what they were after." The award was the biggest recognition they had received, but it was merely icing on the cake, according to the Minners.

"What we do with those kids is from love," D.C. said. "It's not for sale. What we are peddling to these kids is courage–the courage to try! Our specialty is problem kids," he said, "the ones who've been designated 'messups' and are in alternative classes. First we have to engage them in what we're doing. I tell 'em, 'You know some people think you are the messups? Me and Selby are messups, too–one black and one white. We stepped over the line. Some people don't like that. They sent two other messups down here to see if we can surprise them and maybe do something positive with you.' A black male and a white female can pretty much relate to everybody in the room. I'll macho those boys while Selby does what she does. I tell those kids, 'Every one of you is already a winner! Most of those sperms didn't make it. You are the ones that did make it.'

"Most of those kids are very practical. They believe in now. They need information they can use, and see the value in, right away, because they don't have the ability to see the future in longterm information. That's why they're not pursuing an education. By having blinders on and focusing on now, they didn't prepare for the future, and so their future was that they would be in a place like this (alternative school). If you tell them something they can use as soon as they walk out of the classroom, you get more credibility with them. Among the other things, I teach them how to shop, that the most expensive things in the store are probably at eye level. 'Look up,' I say, 'and look down to find the good deals.' They can use that immediately.

"I tell kids they are in a building that was built to make mistakes in," D.C. said. "A school is a safe place to make mistakes. That's the place to make 'em. That's where you ask your questions. Besides, there's no such thing as a mistake, if you learn something from it. I tell them the whole planet is a giant school house, that all of us are really here to learn. If you weren't here to learn, God wouldn't have given you a memory. Every night when you go to sleep, that stuff you learn is filed. And then that makes the 'in' drawer clean. We wake up in the morning and you can now go out there and solve a problem that you were trying to solve the night before. Now you can do it in five minutes. But you've gotta put something in that 'in' drawer. You got to learn something every day.

"You people know you live on a planet, you might have heard that, anyway," the blues singer often told recalcitrant kids in alternative education classes. "You know what that is?" he asked.

"Well, sure, yeah." "We know that." "Sure, Man" are some of the responses he would get.

148

"Our world is called a 'planit' for a reason. If you don't have a plan of your own, stand on the corner out there and see how long it takes before somebody comes along and makes a plan for you! I'm talking about planit. The 'it' I'm talking about is your life!" he said. "You can't live here without being part of a plan. The choice you have to make is, will it be your plan for your life or somebody else's plan.

"Here's how this thing works," he might tell kids he worked with. "We spend our energy and money comes in. If it's your plan, you keep the money and give the world the change. If you don't have a plan for your life, then, when you spend your energy, others get the money and give you the leftover change. If you let somebody else do the planning for you, you might not like what you wind up with," D.C. cautions.

"One of my favorite stories D.C. tells," Selby said, "is when we are sitting in a class of kids with green hair or whatever, and they won't look at us or pay attention. He starts talking to them motivationally, and then he gets to the one about the boat."

"If you wake up in a boat and that boat is moving, you need to try to do something so that you can control the direction of the boat," D.C. said, "because if the boat's moving, it's going downstream. Water does not run uphill. So you are going downstream. You're headed down. You need to start paddlin'. See those berries over on the bank? Pick up that paddle in the bottom of the boat and start paddlin'! You can get to those berries. You don't pick up the paddle and go to work, and you could be getting ready to go over Niagara Falls, if you just sit there in that boat. And you don't have all day to decide. Look for paddles or start paddling with your hands toward what you want, so you can get to the shore safely.

"It depends on the group as to what analogy I use," D.C. said. "If it's a bunch of boys that look like they might be mechanically inclined, I'll use a factual story. If it's more girls, a different story is needed. The message will always be the same, which is to take charge of your life. What they don't understand,

149

most of all, is that the reason they are in alternative school is their fault.

"They'll say, 'Aw, but my family did it. Everybody in my house is a crack addict except me.' But, no, not everybody born into that same situation is in alternative school. Some of those kids chose another route. I tell 'em, 'You just made a bad choice. Life is a series of choices. You didn't trace what you did down the line far enough to see that what you did would land you in here. You don't want to be in here.' I'd tell them their teacher and I were the only ones that want to be here. We made choices to be in there. We made choices to be on the positive side."

Among the ways D.C. taught life lessons was by offering to trade students one of his shiny rings for their shoes. D.C. wore a dozen rings on his right hand when he did a show. They were quite eye-catching to these kids. He told the kids, "I have a bunch of grandkids, and before I left home to come up here, they told me they needed shoes. They want some good tennis shoes; they must be worth at least $50. Now I don't have much money, so I'd like to trade one of these rings for a good pair of sneakers–anybody want to trade?" He always found kids willing to trade. (Hands and even shoes would be waving in the air.) He would then weave a story about knowing the worth of things and about being careful about strangers who offer deals that are too good to be true. He then showed them that his rings were costume jewelry, worth much less than their shoes. He also used the jewelry to give kids hints about behavior that is appropriate to the situations they find themselves in.

"I don't wear this earring in my ear or all these rings on my fingers when I go to the grocery store," he said. "This is my costume I wear on stage, when I'm playing."

When D.C. gave one of his rings to a principal to prove that they were not real diamonds and to use to motivate students, the principal had the whole school writing essays and doing drawings to see who would get to keep D.C.'s ring.

"When you ask a kid, 'What are you doing?' he says, 'Nuthin'.' I say, 'Come here and show me how you do that.' He

150

comes in and stands there. I say, 'Is that nothing?' He says, 'Uhhuh,' I say, 'That's not nothing. You are standing there. I see you. You didn't tell me you were just standing there looking around. You told me you were doing nothing. That ain't nothing.'"

He gets their attention and 'pricks their brains' so they think about what they say and about how they are spending their time. "You can't be standing out on the corner having fun and burnin' the midnight oil to learn something all at the same time," D.C. might say to kids. "You got to sacrifice something."

The Minners pointed out to children that they can get an education not just from school, but from many things, even learning to play music. They learn math when they keep the beat, reading and English when they work on the lyrics, and they learn physics when they learn the explanation of sound waves.

"I tell them play equals fun, so when you play an instrument, you're supposed to be having fun," D.C. said. "Kids get to choose whether they will sing, dance, or play percussion. They vote on songs from a list of 50 kid-appropriate blues and R&B tunes. Songs like 'Blue Suede Shoes,' 'Lean On Me,' 'Respect,' 'My Girl,' 'Stand By Me,' 'Johnny B. Good—we rehearse them, and a great exciting event is created. We make it clear from the start that this is going to be 'fun with music.' We're not trying to create great musicians or singers here. But we are building courage by setting a goal and completing it. These kids will work hard for something they want to do," he said.

With this music and younger students, there will inevitably be lots of wiggling. "We tell them they can get up and dance right on that little spot in front of their seats," Selby said. "We then break into a blues version of 'Hokey Pokey' or 'Itsy Bitsy Spider.' Redoing their songs in blues style gives them a very clear idea of what we are talking about. They dance. Then we say, maybe it's time for them to get a chance to shout in school. Would they like that? 'Yes' comes back across the room... We break into a resounding version of 'Hey, Hey, The Blues Are All

Right.' Imagine three hundred or more kids singing their heads off in a gym!"

"Teachers often have no idea how fourth- or fifth-graders are going to get anything out of the blues," D.C. said in an interview for *Living Blues*, "but what they find out is that there's something in us, and I don't know quite how to put it. But there's a simplicity in us and in our work that the children still possess quite a bit, and to the blues people, too, you still have some of it.. So we relate to each other really well. Sometimes I think it's an Uncle Remus syndrome. Then I realize it transcends that. It's a communication type of thing that me and the children establish. They trust me, first of all, plus I level with them. I let them know right away that I know something that they don't know, and that they might want to know."

Selby often spoke about the incredible love D.C. had for people, treating them with dignity by giving them his attention and respect. He would say "I give them a clean slate. If they act grown they are treated that way. If they don't, I have to treat them that way, too." And so he taught them courage that they could use in all areas of their lives.

"The money we are paid for working with kids is usually spent getting there," D.C. said. "The letters we get from the kids keep us going. When the truck breaks down and I have to walk five miles to get a part, it's thinking about those kids expecting to see us that keeps me going. I gotta get there."

A principal in an elementary school in Rock Island, Illinois, wrote to the Minners, after their appearance there, that their program was "by far the best assembly we've ever had at Longfellow. You wouldn't believe the excitement you created. Again, thank you for providing this wonderful experience for the Longfellow students."

Lola Taylor, writing in the *Guthrie* (Oklahoma) *News Leader*, said, "Students learned of history, legends, inside jokes, the source of 'original tracks,' and about 'faking it.' And, if they really listened, beyond D.C.'s goodnatured wisecracks and the muffle of whispering peers, they got a philosophical lesson on life."

"A kid came backstage at a concert," D.C remembered. "He said, 'Mr. Minner, you changed my life. You came to our school and talked to us and told us about the man in the boat and all that and now I'm a straight-A student. I know what I'm going to do—I'm going to college. He turned to his mother and said 'Tell him, Mom.' She said, 'He's a changed boy. I don't know what you did to him, but it worked.' I told the boy he changed my life, too, which was a big surprise to him. I explained that when I started out on this journey, I said if I could make a difference in one person's life, that would be enough. 'Guess what,' I said to him. 'You are that person–thank you very much!'"

The Minners' influence on children didn't stop with the ones they met through the public school program. It extended beyond to young people of all types and backgrounds through a variety of experiences.

Working With Kids in the Community

"Blues started as front porch music," Selby said. "Having the festival be family friendly is true to the cultural conditions which created it. Kids would be hanging around listening and trying to play drums to it, dancing, or tapping on things. It's a music which is user friendly and inclusive, not exclusive."

Although his grandmother had run a corn whiskey house on the site, D.C. and Selby emphasized family entertainment at their location. Children can't be in the club, which has a license to sell beer, but they are all over the rest of the place during festivals and for music lessons and free jams year-round.

"Did you see those kids running around here last night on this field?" D.C. asked. "The first thing we had to do is turn this from a juke joint into a family event. You do that very slowly around here because these people don't talk to you to ask about what you are doing. They watch you and see what you do."

One of the ways the Minners' encourage families to attend the festival is that kids under 12 are admitted free. Parents

153

without much money to spend can volunteer three hours, including time spent with their own kids in the Kids Village, in exchange for their $15 adult admission and a 50 percent discount on the festival T shirt. D.C.'s wish was that everybody who wanted to be at the festival could be there. He found ways to help that happen.

The Minners have also created scheduled children's activities during Dusk til Dawn Festivals. Not only do children have fun but their parents get to enjoy the music. The Kids Village is open throughout the festivals. Kids get to do hands-on drumming, drum-making, print-making, face-painting, puppets (including a puppet parade across the outdoor dance area), costume play, and music workshops. There is also ample room for kids to move around outdoors on a field where cotton was once grown. Hammocks on trees give them a place to rest.

For most of their years together in Oklahoma, until D.C.'s health deteriorated, the Minners held free music jams twice a month in Rentiesville. Both children and adults were encouraged to spend several hours at a time with two experienced professional musicians who were ready, willing, and able to share their music and their knowhow with all comers. D.C. and Selby cheerfully encouraged and instructed aspiring musicians at all levels of knowledge. Students who stuck with the program got the chance to perform on stage with D.C. and Selby at festivals and other gigs.

"During a residency, once, an eight-year-old little fat kid with freckles came into a room where I was playing piano," D.C. said. "He said he could play. I told him to sit down and play with me. And he did!" D.C. helped, encouraged, and supported the young musician for years. That little boy became Garrett "Big G" Jacobsen, one of the best-known jazz/blues/soul musicians in the Oklahoma City area. In addition, Jacobsen has performed at the Blue Cat Blues Club in Dallas, the Grand Emporium in Kansas City, at the Juneteenth on Greenwood Festival in Tulsa, at the Charlie Christian Jazz Festival in Oklahoma City, and at B.B. King's Blues Club in Hollywood, among other places. "He asked

154

me 'How can I pay you back?'" D.C. said. "I told him, 'When you find somebody as hungry for knowledge as you were, give it to 'em. That would pay me back.' That little fat kid helped another fat kid who went around saying, 'Life sucks!' My kid (Garrett) asked him, 'Why do you say that?' The other kid said, 'If I could play like you do, I wouldn't think life sucks either.' Garrett said, 'I'll teach you.' The other kid had his own band by the time he was seventeen and won the Battle of the Bands at our festival and a trip to the International Blues Challenge in Memphis. It's all about transferring knowledge."

After D.C. died in 2008, Selby revived the tradition of Jam Band, the free blues jams at her home in Rentiesville. She also teaches music there, at libraries, and at other locations in Oklahoma.

(L) A student get acquainted with D.C. and his guitar.

(R) Edmond Summer Arts Camp Sponsored in part by the Oklahoma Arts Council.

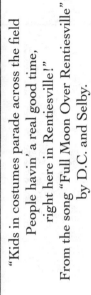

"Kids in costumes parade across the field
People havin' a real good time,
right here in Rentiesville!"
From the song "Full Moon Over Rentiesville"
by D.C. and Selby.

Fun breaks out with kids in Joann McMillan's
costumes at the Blues Fest.

Playing "Piece of my Heart" with the Norman H S
Jazz Band during a residency sponsored by the
Oklahoma Arts Council.

157

B.I.T.S.

Letter: Checotah Elementary   Card: Sadler Arts, Muskogee

A portrait of D.C., drawn by a student who was trying to win his ring. He would leave one at each school.

159

Onstage with Bill Hearn's Chorus, Muskogee High School

Stick puppets and more keep kids having fun as three stages present blues at the Rentiesville Festival. Since 1991, this Festival has put over 500,000 dollars into the pockets of musicians who play this music, with the help of the OAC and many other sponsors. It is a showcase of the Oklahoma Blues Contribution and more, bringing in 200 musicians a year; both international headliners and regionals.

(R) Sculpture after Birdsong painting.

(L) Keith Birdsong Painting

CHAPTER 7: GROWING OLD AND LOVING IT

True reflection on life comes with having lived long enough to have something to reflect on — D.C. lived a long life and had done so much with it. "I would advise everybody to try to get old," D.C. said after his retirement. "I've gotten everything I wanted on this planet. Now I know that sounds ridiculous. I might not have gotten as much as I wanted; I might not have gotten it when I wanted it. But I did get it, and I'm very happy.

"Nobody wishes me harm," he pointed out. "I wish I'd been born fifty years old. The good life began for me about fifty. I had stopped drinking and smoking in my forties, and I had found Selby. Have you noticed bosses are usually forty-five or older? By that time, you've seen the patterns so many times that you have more perspective. It's the business of young people to be giving things up, because that's how the system works.

"In all my life, this is the most perfect time I've ever known, even more so than when I was in the woods alone with those twenty-five pounds of rice and those twenty-five pounds of beans and I could stay in the creative mode twenty-four hours a day," D.C. said. "Now I can do that and not be alone, with twenty-five or thirty years more experience and with a recording studio and ways to document and leave proof of my creativity behind.

"I have to do this. I want to share what I have learned and what I have overcome with my family and with generations to come, because it is all about believing in yourself and investing in yourself. I want everybody to know that they have the seed of greatness. All they have to do is plant it and cultivate it. I want everybody to realize that, if they do that, it will surely bear fruit." D.C. would often startle a new acquaintance by asking, "Do you draw or paint?" The answer was often something like, "No, I don't have any talent for it." "Did you look for it?" D.C. would inquire. "How do you know you don't have it? I didn't start drawing or painting until I was in my fifties."

"I never thought I would be as happy as I am now," he said. "I'm sculpting in bronze. We start off with clay modeling and then go to wax. I'm enjoying this. Just sitting here hour after hour doing this, I hear my grandfather in my head, way back in there, say that I'd better get out and make some money, that sitting here playing with clay dolls is not going to make me a living!"

"But I get to keep telling him, you are wrong. I can now afford to sit here and play with clay dolls and then get up and go play guitar and then go sit at my computer and do some art graphics and then go back in with the clay dolls. I can afford to do this now. I'm 69 years old. If I don't do it now, when am I gonna do it?" D.C. said. "I told my former boss over at the State Arts Council what I'm doing now. He said, 'Oh, so the artist has broken free now!"

As he grew older, D.C. had also proven himself to himself.

"When he got that first Hall of Fame recognition," Selby remembered, "on the way home he said to me, 'I feel like a load has been lifted from my shoulders that I didn't know was even there. My family took so much criticism, raising me in a corn whiskey house. But my grandmother would always say I was gonna be somebody. I feel like I validated the way she raised me when I got inducted. I feel like I finally did that, for her.'" D.C. later was honored in three other halls of fame, besides numerous other honors.

Among the many awards, accolades, and recognition D.C. received, producers of the Oprah Winfrey Show came to Rentiesville to interview D.C. in 1988 in his Down Home Blues Club about his experiences growing up in a black township and then succeeding in a society far different from that.

166

In 1999, the Blues Foundation, which represents 105 blues societies in 27 countries, honored D.C. and Selby in Memphis with their W.C. Handy Education Award for teaching lessons from the blues to kids and including them in their band.

In addition, he was given the State of Oklahoma Governor's Art Award in 2004 as a special recognition for his contributions toward making Oklahoma a better place to live, including creating and maintaining a blues festival that brought as many as seven thousand visitors at a time to his hometown, which has about eighty-five regular residents.

Governor Brad Henry declared September 1, 2006, to be D.C. and Selby Minner Day in the State of Oklahoma in recognition for their "leadership abilities demonstrated in their natural gentle styles and caring natures," for dedicating their lives to spreading the joyful sound of the blues around the world, for creating the Dusk til Dawn Blues Festival,' founded in 1991, complete with adult workshops and children's educational activities, for housing the Oklahoma Blues Hall of Fame" and for numerous other contributions listed on the proclamation.

Loving Communities

As much as Minner appreciated all those honors, the one that touched him most deeply was that the people in his hometown changed the name of the street he lived on to DC Minner Street. His family had once been outcasts in that religious town because his grandmother ran a corn whiskey house.

When D.C. was in his fifties, he and Selby started a volunteer fire department in his town and continued to support it into his seventies. He campaigned successfully for the state to install a warning light at an unmarked crossing where school buses and other vehicles had to cross a railroad track in his community. He and Selby organized and participated in regular free jams and workshops to encourage both children and adults to develop their musical skills. He did innumerable benefits and fund raisers for worthy causes in many places, and often cooked meals for

167

senior citizens into his seventies. He said "whatever you sell, you have to give some of it away."

In fact, the Rentiesville alumni association presented a certificate to D.C., recognizing the contribution his grandmother Lura had made to that community. Although Lura was ostracized through much of her lifetime, she nevertheless had provided an informal after-school facility where children were welcomed to come and play while their parents worked. Lura was a businesswoman, and she mentored numerous young people by exposing them to experiences that went beyond farming, the occupation of most parents at that time, in that place.

"Having those people name a street after me was a way of saying, 'Sorry, we had you wrong'," Minner said. "They remember when I was still messing up, and they did not name any streets after themselves. Others who give me awards know of me but the people in Rentiesville know me. That means a whole lot to me. It also meant redemption for my grandmother." It meant they knew Lura had raised him well, despite her circumstances.

"Life is an emotional experience," D.C. said. "Enjoying those emotions is what I want to do now. You shouldn't have to turn your whole life into only a logical experience where everything you do is done because you have to make money. That's what I'd had to do all those years. I'd come into this studio or become involved in an art project, then I'd have to stop because I knew I had to go play music to pay the bills. Before my retirement, I never got to create for more than a few days a year. Then I'd have to go do a residency or a gig so that I could pay my bills.

"I'm now retired, officially, but I haven't stopped playing music. My guitar is more important to me now than it ever was before in my life. The key word in that statement is 'me,' because now I play only for myself. I play every day, and I feel more obligated now to play than ever. I used to play for the girls, for the social connections, to buy me a drink—all that stuff. I'm not playing for that now. I sit here on my couch and I play for me.

"I have an obligation, since I've been entrusted with this talent, to develop it to its highest potential. That has nothing to do with money. It has nothing to do with fame. It is only between the guitar and myself. I have to see just how good I can become on that guitar. This would be the worst possible time to stop playing the guitar. Well, maybe tomorrow would be worse, because I'd have one more day invested. But, after investing so much time and so much energy and so much effort, it would be a terrible, terrible time for me to let all that evaporate.

"That's one of the reasons I have to keep playing guitar," D.C. said. "Another one is that I have two Hall of Fame trophies sitting in there on my counter: one from the Oklahoma Jazz Hall of Fame and one from the Oklahoma Music Hall of Fame. I have another trophy in the house for our work in education from the International Blues Foundation. Selby and I share that one; that one covers the United States and twenty-six foreign countries. I'm in the Oklahoma Blues Hall of Fame. I am very proud of those trophies. I have a street sign out there that says D.C. Minner Street. I'm very proud of that. But my grandmother always taught me not to rest on your laurels, but to keep doing, so that's what I'm doing.

"That's very, very comfortable for me. Getting into that," he said, "I want to produce a lot more music. I want to produce a lot of sculpture pieces. When you stop learning, that's when you start dying. That's when you really get old. I'm not ready to die. I've got too much stuff I want to do.

"That's where I am right now. I'm very content. I'm so happy that I'm getting to finish out the cycle of getting old. I think the going out will be very beautiful. I feel very lucky, very privileged and very proud of myself for having made it to this satisfying position from where I started."

The Peace, Love and Happiness Tour

D.C. spent his last happy years in the same location where he was born and raised.

"I joined the army to get away from here," he said. "That's how bad I wanted to leave. Later I would have been willing to fight off an army to get back here. Selby and I enjoy this house. This is our world. We know the rest of the people are out there, but we are busy here. I love this place because I can relax here. I can be me. The people around us already know who I am. There's no need to try to be anybody else to please others. I can go barefoot here.

"I can do my trip here. We all know each other," he pointed out. "Shoot, we're probably all cousins. I lost both kidneys and then had a heart attack during our annual festival. I've been in bed for a year and a half. I get up and do a gig and then go right back to bed."

Carl Gustafson, music producer and lead singer in Blind Dog Smokin, witnessed the spectacle of the spell D.C. Minner could cast, even as a senior citizen. "I met D.C. Minner in the day-lit interior of his home from birth, also known as the Down Home Blues Club in Rentiesville, Oklahoma, a tiny black community, hidden from the main roads.

"A gaunt figure with a nappy gray head and stringy goatee, he mumbled through toothless gums trying to wake himself into sociability. He appeared many years older than his official age. It was hard to detect where the worn upholstery of his old chair melded into his disheveled clothes, so homogenous were the artifacts of his life throughout this old juke joint he called home."

Later, Gustafson saw D.C. perform. "I saw his eyes. Bright eyes, black and eerie in the smoky room. Rings adorned his every finger and thumb. The stance was proud, the visage was stone. The smile? Slow and chilling. The eyes turned toward me under a flat-brimmed hat, focused from their corners now, piercing the haze to meet mine. Did that man know me? Uneasy, I leaned forward to study the dark figure slow-stepping in the interior dusk. Something familiar limned into my memory, then vanished. The gray cloth of his suit hung elegantly from the lank frame. An aura was distinctly about him as he moved like an old panther, sure of his lair. I thought I knew him, then I thought I did not. 'Who is he?' I wondered. 'What is he?' Suddenly I knew. I was beholding a Doppelganger..."

"D.C. is a storyteller," Gustafson said, "one of the two best raconteurs alive. It was he that had introduced me to the Doppelganger. 'I put a hat on him and a fine suit,' he had said in third-person narrative. 'I put in his teeth — the ladies don't want no gummy man singin' to 'em, and I git his rings 'n shit, shiny shoes, an' a red shirt. He is a struttin' man when I bring him out . . .'

"What the hell was he talking about? Bring who out? I hadn't fully understood until that night when I hadn't recognized the transformation of D.C. Minner himself. So concerted had been the metamorphosis that I had to percolate my vision in order to change my preconception. Was it really that tired and dusty old man, now staring in defiance and triumph as he galvanized the night air with his electric guitar and marched about in a soul-strut born and raised on a thousand stages like this one? 'I'll be damned,' I had muttered."

Gustafson further suggested, "People fall in love with doppelgangers, not knowing that they only live when performing, and then, as D.C. explained it, '. . . I put him back away until it's time to bring him out again.'" It may be that only Selby and Lura understood D.C. better than Gustafson did.

D.C. and Selby did their last tour together, a repeat of their many trips to the West Coast, in 2006. The "Peace, Love and Happiness Tour" was six weeks long, included fourteen four-hour gigs, and D.C. did not miss a note. He was seventy-one, on dialysis, and in poor health at the time. But, on the way out of Oklahoma for the last time, he said, "I'm so happy right now. I've got a good group of musicians who trust me and want to go with me. This is the very first time I've ever got to go in a nice vehicle and with enough money. I'm at peace."

D.C.'s last years were beautiful, in part, because he never quit learning, never stopped trying, and never stopped counting his blessings. "I tell my family not to feel sorry for me, as I'll be getting a release someday soon," D.C. said near the end of his life. "Mama Lura used to say to me, 'you don't know how to leave well enough alone!'" D.C. recalled. "Now I have learned it —how to leave well enough alone."

Triumph

Despite never having had a "hit" record, D.C. was inducted into the Oklahoma Music Hall of Fame along with people much better known to the public than he was, including country superstar Ronnie Dunn of Brooks & Dunn. Nevertheless, D.C. stole the spotlight by giving the best acceptance speech of the night, by getting the first laugh of the night, by getting the first standing ovations (a total of four) of the night, and by creating excitement and enthusiasm in the standing-room-only audience, most of whom had not previously known him or his music.

D.C. never stopped giving, right up to the end. Selby relates that, "He spent three of the last four years he lived in bed. He would spend all week building up energy to go play music. Then it would take a day for him to recover from a gig. But when he was performing, he would get complete relief from his illness. The music would take him away. He lived on to be with me and to be able to play."

Even when he was bedridden, he received visitors eagerly and graciously. He hid nothing from his past and was willing to share his hard-earned knowledge. He tried, in every way he could think of, to pass along the lessons he had learned and to help others avoid his mistakes. No effort was too great, no embarrassment too severe, no humiliation was too hurtful to get in the way of his determination to leave something worthwhile behind when he left this life.

One of D.C.'s many loving gifts to Selby was that he prepared her to keep performing and to keep producing the Dusk Til Dawn Blues Festival after he was gone. With D.C. coaching, Selby worked to go from playing bass to being able to play lead guitar when necessary to keep her band working. In addition, the couple created a nonprofit corporation, Friends of Rentiesville Blues, Inc. Working with the board members of that organization, Selby has been able to successfully organize and produce the festival every year since D.C.'s death in 2008.

D.C. had very few regrets. "If I had it to do over, I'd probably do it much the same, except that I'd start earlier, and I wouldn't get drunk so much. That was not necessary." D.C. Minner died at age 73 a satisfied and happy man. "D.C. said he wanted to die with his eyes open," Selby recalled. "He said, 'I don't want to miss it; I want to SEE death coming!'"

He died at home in his own bed, just as he wanted to do. "It was very peaceful," Selby said. "D.C. was a very mental and spiritual cat, as you know," Selby said. "He accepted it when he lost the ability to walk or to get up or even to roll over without help. I could lie down next to him, and we would start talking; great memories. I still had my best friend, and he still had his best friend.

"Near the end," she said, "I was having a conversation with Tiki, a friend who lives nearby, about going into town to a grocery store. Tiki helped me every day. D.C. at that time realized he was unable to keep up with that conversation, and he was gone in three or four days after that." Selby said D.C. was unwilling to continue to live after he became aware that he was not comprehending all that was going on around him. "He would not do that to himself and he wouldn't do it to me," Selby said.

"I've been told there are two things musicians look for–wealth and immortality," D.C. said in his later years. He told Selby a story about famed blind jazz sax player Rahsaan (Roland Kirk), who was famous in the nineteen sixties for being able to play several instruments at once. "He would carry his horns, some of which were homemade and held together with rubber bands and duct tape, in a duffle bag," Selby recalled D.C. telling her. "Since Rahsaan could not see, D.C. would take his arm when he saw him head across a street. One day Rahsaan stopped and just looked at D.C. 'What do you want out of life?'" he asked. Surprised, D.C. said, 'I don't know.' 'That's a lie,' Rahsaan responded. 'You want fame and fortune, just like all other musicians. Well, I've GOT fame and fortune, and I don't need YOU pulling me across the street!' D.C. said, I never touched him again."

"I've been playing music for more than 50 years and haven't got the fortune yet," D.C. said in his later years. "So I'm trying to cash in on immortality by getting kids focused on something that will bring them success and happiness. If any of these kids get started in the blues, they will remember that old black man with the rings who came to the school and showed them how it was done, and I'll be alive as long as they remember me."

Betty Price, former Executive Director of the Oklahoma State Arts Council said about D.C., "I admire him tremendously not only for his lifetime commitment to the blues community and to the genre, but also because he has changed the lives of everyone he has touched. His legacy will live on for generations to come."

"This mortal and mysterious life we have all happened upon has obvious risks, like death, dismemberment, blindness, disease, poverty, war, rape and subjugation," said Carl Gustafson, the music producer who recognized D.C.'s Doppelganger persona, "and subtler but equally vital risks, like humiliation, defeat, embarrassment, ridicule and the despair from lost hope. If you knew the rollercoaster could not wreck and that even if it did, you were immortal and couldn't be hurt in any way, it wouldn't take any courage to ride it, and it follows that the exhilaration would be greatly diminished.

"I couldn't help but wonder after my marvelous morning with D.C.," Gustafson said, "what the world would be like if the Doppelganger in all of us was allowed to live. What wondrous adventures we could share."

D.C. Returns to the "Hot Dog Stand on Telegraph"
in Berkeley where he lived in the 70's.

Mayor Mildred Burkhalter renames part of the Texas Trail, formerly
known as 11th Street, as D.C. Minner Street—his fave award!

Blues

D.C. & Selby Minner

interviewed by Jacques Depoorten

Lowell Fulson, Jay McShann, Claude Williams, Jimmy Noler, Jimmy Rushing, Joe & Jimmy Liggins and Roy Milton do all hav one thing in common they were al born in the state of Oklahoma an they all started their musical career there. In search for greater fame, al of them moved to cities in othe states such as Kansas City und Lo Angeles. That may be the mail reason why Oklahoma does no have the same magic amon, bluedovers as Mississippi, Texas o Louisiana. Undeservedly so, becaus up to the present day, Oklahom has a blues tradition that is kep alive by younger players as well a by veteran musicians. One sucl veteran is guitarist/singer D.C Minner. Playing mostly locall; during the fifties, he was the bass guitarist in the road bands of som of the greatest names in blues rhythm & blues and black rock & roll during the sixties. In the earl; seventies he switched to the guitar With his wife Selby, who is also the bass-guitarist and a featured singe: in his band "Blues On The Move", he is living in his birthplace Rentiesville (Population : 75). Since 1988 D.C. & Selby are running there "The Down Home Blues Club", an authentic juke joint. In 1991 they started the annual "Dusk 'til Dawn Blues Festival" featuring some of the best national and local acts. D.C. & Selby also travel the state of Oklahoma performing in schools to teach the students. In the Winter of 1994 they were touring Europe. Their temporary home during this tour was in Ostend, Belgium where I could interview D.C. & Selby at length about their own fascinating careers and the blues scene in Oklahoma.

Oklahoma

The Blues Life Journal   Ausland, Norway

D.C. Signs the poster of his Oklahoma
Jazz Hall of Fame Induction 1999

D.C. , Selby and the band play on New Year's Eve for
Opening Night in OKC at the Stage Center

All packed up and ready to roll.

Load in time at the Jambalya in Arcata CA
Andy helps Hiram (drummer, keyboard)
and girlfriend Suzy Abbott.

Brother-in-Law Ron Conley reads about the up coming
"Boot Scootin' Induction" at the Oklahoma Music Hall of Fame.

Selby's mom, Dortha Guenther Mershon and her sister, Jean.

Rehearsal night in Muskogee for OMHOF Inductions.

Ron & Hilary Conley, Dortha (Selby's Mom), Selby and D.C.

D.C. Shines at the pre induction party as LaNelda looks on.
At the Down Home Blues Club.

Tiki and Harry Blackwell

**Lifelong friends gather; for the
Oklahoma Music Hall of Fame Induction**

DW, Michael "Tiki" Teague, Janie

D.C. prepares to be inducted into the Oklahoma Music Hall of Fame in 2003. He always said he wished his partner/bassist/wife could have been inducted with him. He would say "You have made every step with me all the way. I couldn't have done it without you...you should be getting in here too." (Photo: Selby Minner)

D.C. Minner and Flash Terry
Induction Performance OMHOF

End of the song "Hideaway" at the Civic Center in Muskogee, OK
OMHOF Inductions 2003

Shortly after this induction, D.C. decided to found the Blues Hall of
Fame in Rentiesville at Down Home Blues Club which he had
created from the family Homestead. He said, "We need to create a
Blues Hall of Fame. We have a little place — there are too many, and
they are going to miss some of 'em.. and we know everybody, and we
need to get them on the wall while they are still alive." There are now
over 100 inductees in the OBHOF.

Opinion

Muskogee Daily Phoenix · Wednesday, July 2, 2003 · Section A, Page 7

EDITORIALLY SPEAKING

Minner's Hall induction well-deserved

D.C. Minner is a local legend. He has been working with children for years, teaching them an appreciation for a uniquely American form of music.

Minner, an extraordinary blues guitarist, will be inducted into the Oklahoma Music Hall of Fame this year.

It's a long overdue recognition, as far as we're concerned.

Minner has ripped it up with some of the best musicians in the world, but he makes his home here, and he's committed to seeing music grow and be appreciated in this area, working with an annual blues festival, teaching appreciation at schools and other activities.

His music is certainly something to behold. Along with his bass guitarist wife, Selby, Minner's blues is top-notch stuff.

But his legacy to Oklahoma music and more particularly to the Muskogee area's rich music history will be that he didn't keep his talent to himself, hoarding huge **Minner** buckets of cash and living the rock star lifestyle — something he certainly could have chosen and been successful at.

Instead, after a successful touring career, he moved back to his native Rentiesville with his wife.

The Minners equate this most recent recognition with having "made it."

Selby Minner said it best: "In Memphis, they know of him. Here, they know him."

For a child who heard his first live music from acoustic guitars because there was no electricity, Minner has grown into a

man who has made his living doing what he loves: "Play the music."

We hope more young musicians will take Minner's example and give back to their communities, sharing the love for music that brings pleasure to all.

Music is one of the things that separates man from the animals — the ability to appreciate such an abstract and ethereal thing as notes flying through the air.

Legends like Minner help us appreciate even more the music that gave birth to Rock and Roll and gave a voice to the concerns and triumphs of regular people.

Blues is one of music's more expressive and honest incarnations, and Minner is one of its finest musicians.

We congratulate Minner on his upcoming induction, and we applaud the hall of fame for recognizing local greatness.

190

To the victor belongs the Made in Oklahoma spoils! Thanks OMHOF!

D.C. receives Governor's Arts Award presented by
OAC Director and friend, Betty Price.

D.C. and famed Rentiesville Historian Dr. John Hope Franklin
receive Governor's Arts Awards in OKC. Note the guitar and
drumset — D.C. and Selby got to perform at the event!
Dr. Franklin is a Rentiesville native with 150 honorary degrees!

The Oklahoman from OKC
comes to do a story, and
New York Times comes
in for an interview (right).

Texas Road Recording Company in action:
D.C. moves the Roland Digital Recorder
to Mount Olive Star Baptist Church to record a live CD

D.C. Minner at his Blues Festival.
Tulsa World photo, used with permission.

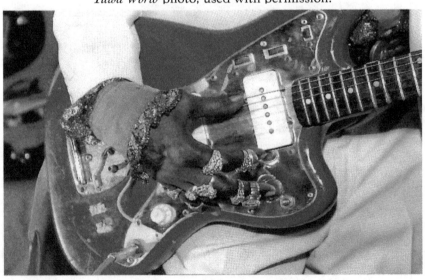

D.C. Sets up sound on
the Back Porch Stage

Tiki,
a great friend
and volunteer

D.C. shows us how to be
cool even after we get old...

Above: D.C. on tour in Berkeley. Photo by Joan Bobkoff.

PHOTO© GABY GUYMAN

At the world famous Cains Ballroom in Tulsa sitting in with
Grammy winner & friend Lucinda Williams

Here's what I love about Musicians Ladies and Gentlemen. I played at The Blues Hall of fame inductions and the place was packed. I'm talking wait ten minutes at the front door just to go outside!!!! Anyway we finished our set and the next band is standing there before we even got off stage with all their equipment on stage totally blocking us from even getting us and our stuff off stage. One of th... anyway I end up leaving my snare stand and my whole stick bag and it's worth easily $500.00 with sticks, brushes, Mallets, bamboo "soft sticks' Etc. and in the morning I'm tripping when I realize what I had done. So I drive there this afternoon to see what was left and my stand and whole stick bag full of stuff were sitting there waiting for me on an empty clean stage. Not one thing missing!!! And there were soooooo many musicians playing there. My point? Musicians would never steal from another musician. We all realize we make little to no money (For what we are worth... LOL) and there's so much respect. For everyone who played that night and "Bear" who's kit we used thank you for being so great as musicians and fellow human beings. And again - you and DC created and nurtured a very special "venue" for lack of a better word that feels so welcoming and friendly. The "Down Home Blues Club" is awesome and has become a home for me where I know we can go be at home and JAM!!!! Thanks again Musicians for making me realize how cool we really are.... Hammer

D.C. Minner
1935 - 2008
www.dcminnerblues.com

photo: Richard Byrd

People Important to the Story of D.C.'s Life

The extended Minner family, in the order they are mentioned.

Selby Guenther Minner: blues musician, songwriter, teacher, author

Clark Martin: called Doctor Clark Martin, D.C.'s great, great grandfather after whom D.C. was named. Clark Martin was a pharmacist and a businessman who was recruited in 1900 by Indian Territory officials to move from Alabama to the area that later became Oklahoma.

Ann Martin: D.C.'s great-great grandmother, a Cherokee Indian married to a black man, which affected where they would be allowed to live together

Lura Eufaula Gaye Martin Pearson Drennan: D.C.'s grandmother who reared him. She was Clark's and Ann's granddaughter, brought with them to Indian Territory in an effort to find a better life than was possible for blacks in Alabama after the Civil War.

Tom Pearson: Lura's first husband and father of her three daughters: Ethel, Helen (D.C.'s mother) and Elsie. Pearson deserted the family during the Great Depression.

Charlie Drennan: Lura's second husband, D.C.'s step-grandfather who helped to rear him. Drennan was a World War I veteran. His pension check was the first regular income Lura had ever known. It helped her to start a business which finally ended the threat of starvation for her family. D.C. called Drennan his "protector" in a family otherwise made up of very strong and assertive women.

Helen Pearson Minner: Lura's daughter, D.C.'s mother who gave birth to him at the age of 17

Clarence Minner: D.C.'s father, whose marriage to D.C.'s mother lasted only about six weeks. He moved to California and was not around when D.C. was growing up.

Elsie Pearson: D.C.'s "baby auntie," Lura's youngest child who, at the age of 14, had the day-to-day responsibility for D.C.'s care. Elsie took D.C. to community dances with her and gave him his first taste of music.

Ethel Pearson DeBouse: Lura's oldest daughter, D.C.'s aunt who kept the home place going until D.C. finally returned to Oklahoma to take his place as the head of the family.

Doris Morris Haynes Minner: D.C.'s high school music teacher who kept him after school to practice music. After D.C.'s time in the military, Doris became his first wife.

Tony Minner: D.C.'s son, a computer science graduate who installed and maintained the computer system on the Air Force One used by President Bill Clinton, among other high-level assignments. Tony was a talented musician, first-chair saxophone player in the winner of an all state band contest. He had a partial music scholarship to college, but did not pursue music after he graduated from college. Tony died in 2010; he had never reconciled with his father after blaming D.C. for his divorce from Doris. Tony married four times and fathered five children.

Sheila Minner Huntington: D.C.'s daughter and a graduate of The University of Oklahoma. Sheila worked for many years at the O.U. student loan office. She has worked with Selby to keep the Dusk Til Dawn blues festivals going after D.C.'s death in 2008.

Relfus Bobo Haynes: D.C.'s stepson. D.C. married his mother, Doris, when Bobo was five and D.C. regarded Bobo as his son. One of D.C.'s most haunting songs, "Blues for Bobo," was written after Bobo committed suicide in 2003. D.C. was so strongly affected by Bobo's death that he was never able to perform the song in public. He recorded it in the privacy of his studio.

Linda Minner: Tony's first wife, mother of D.C.'s first grandchild Erica

Angela Minner Kastel: Tony's second wife, mother of Micaela and Danielle

Dalcia Ortiz Minner: Tony's last wife, mother of Tony Minner, Junior, and Christopher Minner.

Selby's family members who are important to the story, in the order they are mentioned

Dortha Selby Guenther Mershon: Selby's mother

Jean Marie Guenther Johnson Stuhlmann: Selby's sister, a counselor

Other People Who Influenced D.C.'s Life

Sam Durham: a gambler/street person/exconvict who showed Lura how to make Choctaw beer from readily-available ingredients, giving her a way to earn enough money to feed her family. Some members of Durham's family were musicians who influenced D.C. to learn music. One of his sons, L.D. Durham, was a piano player who was about 18 when D.C. was a toddler. L.D. sat D.C. on his lap while he played the piano. In D.C.'s later years, he was amazed that he still remembered L.D.'s arrangements of some songs, including "Trouble in Mind."

Eugene Edwards D.C.'s California guru, who taught him life skills, including religions, philosophies, Yogananda, numerology, and astrology. Edwards was a jazz guitarist who recorded with Groove Holmes. He played on the great hit, "Misty".

Johnny B. Ellis,: a musician who worked at the Veterans' Administration Hospital in Oklahoma City where D.C. worked as a medical technician after his military service. Ellis invited D.C. to go to gigs with him and eventually to sit in on performances. Ellis was married to "Miss Blues," Dorothy Ellis, a Hall of Fame blues/jazz musician who was friends with D.C. for the remainder of his life.

Arturo Jacobs : army buddy who taught D.C. to play guitar

Melvin "Tank" Jernigan: an Oklahoma musician from OKC. Played with Larry Johnson and D.C. in the New Breed. He had a lot of connections and helped D.C. break into the music scene in California in the late 60's. Jernigan worked for Capitol Records and did horn arrangements for Ray Charles. He played flute on Canned Heat's megahit "Goin to the Country."

"Coach" Marshall: a tough industrial arts teacher and basketball coach who saw that D.C. had potential and who forced D.C. to give his best efforts in school and in other activities.

Tony Mathews: a Checotah, Oklahoma, musician who helped D.C. to break into the music scene in California in the late 60's. Mathews traveled extensively as Ray Charles' guitarist for 18 years and also worked with Little Richard for two years. D.C. referred to Tony as one of the best guitar players in the world.

Bo Jones: five years older than D.C., Bo was an accomplished pianist and a popular band leader. He encouraged D.C. to stick with music and included D.C. in a singing group he formed, the Five Clouds of Joy. A photo of Five Clouds of Joy is included in this book. Three of the five from that Rentiesville group became professional musicians.

Altonia Ferguson Nutter: Doris Haynes Minner's great-aunt. Altonia was called "Sister" by the family. She reared D.C.'s children after Doris died. She was an educated woman, a school principal, and was highly respected in the community, serving as the town's treasurer. She was also a seamstress, and traveled around the world. She died in 1993. The last time Tony Minner came back to Rentiesville was to attend her funeral.

Grant Smith: the first black male D.C. knew who owned his own businesses, including providing a jukebox in Lura's club after electricity came to Rentiesville. Smith was a mentor to the young D.C. who was growing up surrounded by women. D.C. learned, from Smith's employees, how to work on both cars and radios. Those skills contributed to D.C.'s successes in later life.

Janie Teague Urbach: a dear friend from California who had worked in the bar where D.C. and Selby met. She moved to Oklahoma in 2003 to be near the Minners.

Michael "Tiki" Urbach-Teague: a very close friend to the Minners who also worked in the Odyssey bar where the Minners met in 1972. Tiki and Janie moved to Oklahoma during D.C.'s last years. They had been driving from California frequently to work with the Minners on the festivals. Tiki and Janie were invaluable in helping Selby cope during D.C.'s final illness.

Claude Williams: Oklahoma musician who helped D.C. to break into the music scene in California in 1969. He toured with Ike and Tina Turner playing trumpet and coronet for many years. OBHOF inductee.

CPSIA information can be obtained
at www.ICGtesting.com
Printed in the USA
FFHW02n1022141018
48789297-52925FF